8/18

EXPLORING SPACE

For my brother, Edmund
M. J.

For James and Daniel
S. B.

Text copyright © 2017 by Martin Jenkins

Illustrations copyright © 2017 by Stephen Biesty

First U.S. edition 2017

Library of Congress Catalog Card Number pending

ISBN 978-0-7636-8931-5

17 18 19 20 21 22 CCP 10 9 8 7 6 5 4 3 2 1

Printed in Shenzhen, Guangdong, China

This book was typeset in Futura and Adobe Caslon Pro.

The illustrations were done in pencil and colored pencil.

Candlewick Press

99 Dover Street

Somerville, Massachusetts 02144

visit us at www.candlewick.com

EXPLORING SPACE
FROM GALILEO TO THE MARS ROVER AND BEYOND

MARTIN JENKINS • illustrated by STEPHEN BIESTY

CANDLEWICK PRESS

CONTENTS

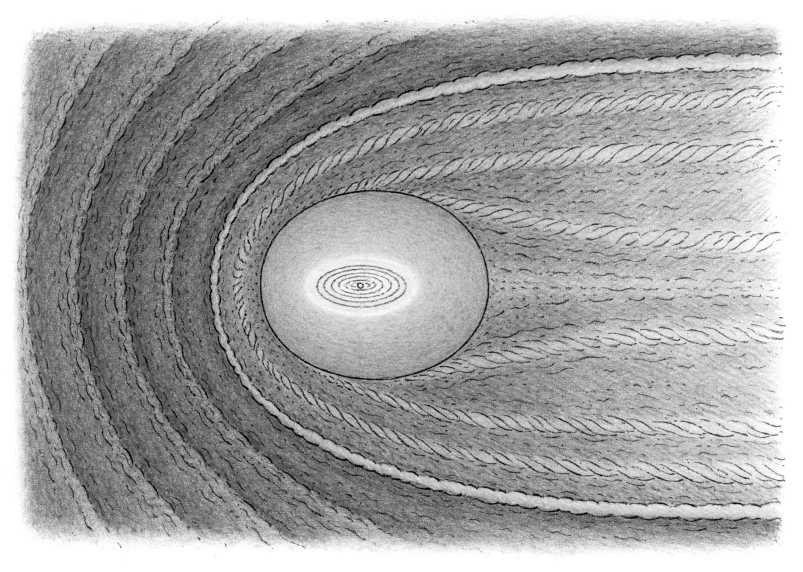

Our solar system is like an enormous bubble in space with the sun at its center. The edge of this bubble is called the heliopause.

THE SOLAR SYSTEM . . . AND BEYOND

Monday September 5, 1977, seemed like a normal working day at the US Air Force Space Launch Complex at Cape Canaveral in Florida. A *Titan IIIE Centaur* rocket was due to be launched at noon. There was nothing unusual about this—hundreds of rockets had been launched here in the previous twenty years. Nor did there seem to be anything particularly special about the load the rocket was carrying: no humans, not even any animals. Just an unmanned spacecraft about the size of a grand piano, weighing 1,797 pounds (722 kilograms)

and equipped with cameras and sensors, some computers (utterly feeble by today's standards), three small nuclear-battery power generators, and a radio system, including a 12-foot- (3.7-meter-) diameter dish antenna, folded up like an outsize umbrella for takeoff. There was one odd thing, though. Attached to the outside of the spacecraft was a gold-plated copper phonograph record in an aluminum case. Engraved on the record were sound recordings and more than one hundred encoded photos. On its cover were some odd-looking symbols.

A STARRY MESSENGER

The most distant man-made object ever, *Voyager 1* is just at the start of an epic journey across the Milky Way. In about 40,000 years, it should pass within 1.6 light years — that's 9.4 trillion miles — of a star known by astronomers as AC+79 3888, still carrying messages from twentieth-century humanity engraved on its Golden Record.

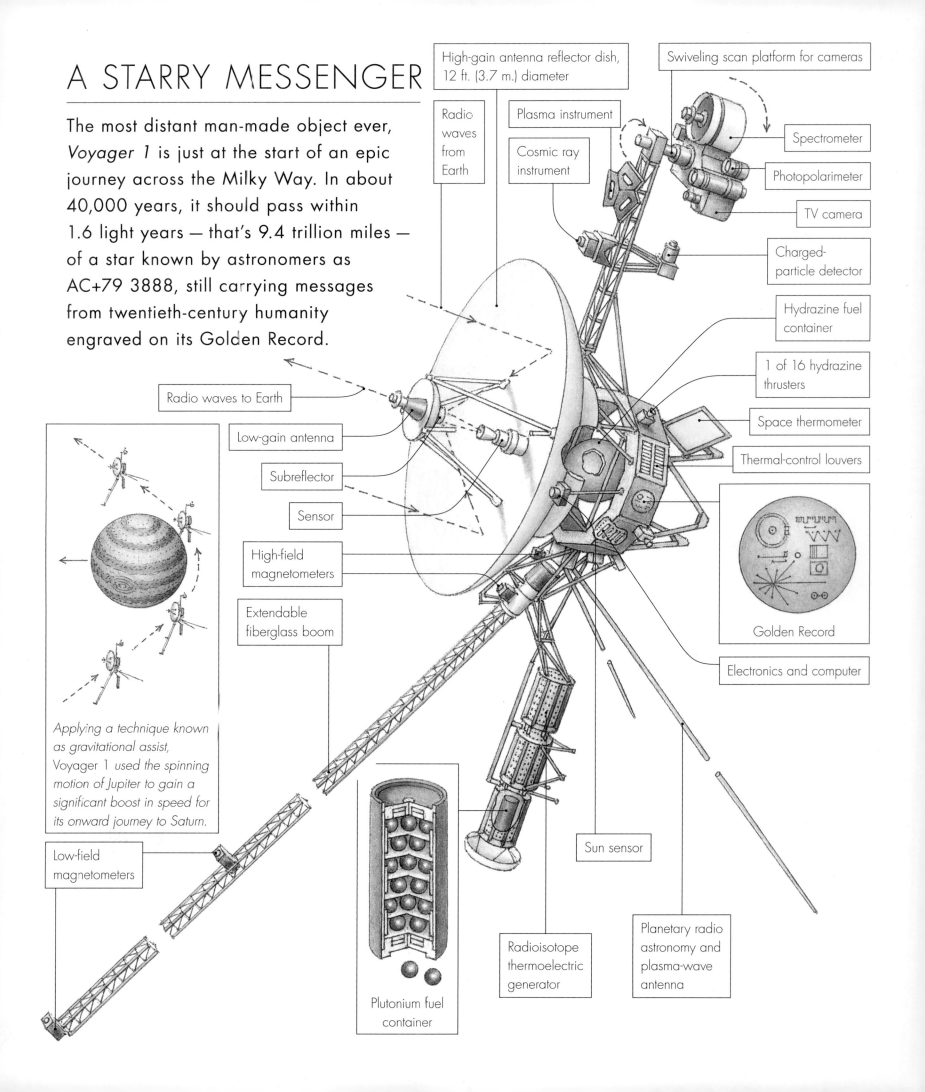

High-gain antenna reflector dish, 12 ft. (3.7 m.) diameter

Swiveling scan platform for cameras

Radio waves from Earth

Plasma instrument

Cosmic ray instrument

Spectrometer

Photopolarimeter

TV camera

Charged-particle detector

Hydrazine fuel container

1 of 16 hydrazine thrusters

Space thermometer

Thermal-control louvers

Radio waves to Earth

Low-gain antenna

Subreflector

Sensor

High-field magnetometers

Golden Record

Electronics and computer

Extendable fiberglass boom

Applying a technique known as gravitational assist, Voyager 1 used the spinning motion of Jupiter to gain a significant boost in speed for its onward journey to Saturn.

Low-field magnetometers

Plutonium fuel container

Radioisotope thermoelectric generator

Sun sensor

Planetary radio astronomy and plasma-wave antenna

The presence of the record was a hint that this was no ordinary rocket launch. In fact, it was to be the start of the most epic voyage yet undertaken from planet Earth. Almost thirty-five years later, still operating and still sending information back to Earth, the spacecraft—*Voyager 1*—crossed an invisible boundary called the heliopause and passed into interstellar space, leaving the known planets of the solar system far behind. The distance it had covered to do this is mind-boggling—11.2 billion miles (18 billion kilometers), about 120 times as far as the earth to the sun.

Voyager 1's journey has been more successful than anyone dared hope. Its original mission was to explore the mysterious giant planets whose orbits lie far out in the solar system. In the 1960s, scientists had figured out that during the 1970s all four of these—Jupiter, Saturn, Uranus, and Neptune—would be lined up in such a way that using a technique called gravitational assist, a spacecraft would be able to pass by them all in turn.

This was a rare opportunity, as the planets would not line up in the same way for another 175 years. The US National Aeronautics and Space Administration (NASA), which was behind the project, had at first wanted to send several space probes out to take advantage of this alignment, but that turned out to be too expensive. In the end, NASA did manage to persuade the government to provide enough money for two probes, rather than just one, although the missions planned for each were different. *Voyager 2* would try to visit all four large planets. *Voyager 1,* its identical twin but traveling on a more direct course, would visit just Jupiter and Saturn.

Voyager 2 actually took off first, on August 20, but by the end of the year, *Voyager 1* had overtaken it. For the next fifteen months, it zipped through space, heading directly for Jupiter, the largest planet in the solar system. In March 1979, it flew to within 130,000 miles (207,000 kilometers) of the giant planet's surface, before plunging even deeper into space on its way to Saturn. It reached there in November 1980, flying past a number of Saturn's many moons, all the while sending photographs

and information from its sensors back to Earth. Its main mission successfully completed, *Voyager 1* continued on its journey. Its role now was to explore the outer reaches of the solar system for as long as its power supply lasted and its instruments kept working.

Some nine months after *Voyager 1* had visited Saturn, *Voyager 2* arrived there, on its way to the even more distant Uranus and Neptune. It took another four and a half years to reach Uranus, and another three and a half after that to get to Neptune. Then it too went on its way, heading away from the sun in a different direction from *Voyager 1.*

It's hard to say when exactly the *Voyager*s or any of the other three spacecraft currently on track to leave the solar system (*Pioneers 10* and *11,* launched in the early 1970s, and *New Horizons,* launched in 2006) will have left it completely behind. That's because we can't really say exactly where the solar system ends. The heliopause is one kind of edge, but the sun's gravity continues to have an effect much farther away than that. Astronomers are pretty sure that way, way beyond the heliopause is a region called the Öpik-Oort cloud, where billions of objects, some many miles across, are endlessly circling the sun, in the same way as our own planet but in hugely bigger orbits. The edge of this cloud can be thought of as another kind of edge of the solar system. Even speeding along at 38,000 mph (60,000 kph), *Voyager 1* will take about 30,000 years to reach there. By then it will long ago have stopped working—after around 2025, its batteries will not be strong enough to power any of its instruments—but there's no reason it should not still be intact and still traveling on its solitary journey through the outer reaches of the galaxy.

It's an amazing thought: less than a hundred years after the invention of the car, we humans have launched vehicles that can leave the solar system. Not only that, but we've also landed space probes on two planets, two moons, two asteroids, and a comet, and visited one of those moons—the earth's own—in person, not once, but six times. No wonder people call this the space age.

OUR OWN BACKYARD

The solar system is quite a busy place. Eight planets, including Earth, orbit the sun in slightly stretched circles called ellipses, each taking a different length of time — from 88 days to 165 years — to make one circuit.

Many other objects go around the sun: asteroids, some of them hundreds of miles across, concentrated in a belt between Mars and Jupiter; comets on highly eccentric orbits, swooping in from the outer reaches of the solar system and then heading away again; and, just beyond Neptune, the Kuiper Belt, containing Pluto and other dwarf planets.

All the planets, except Mercury and Venus, have their own natural satellites — moons and moonlets that in turn orbit them. The earth has just one; Mars two; Saturn dozens, as well as a series of spectacular icy rings that can be seen from Earth.

Outer Planets

| NEPTUNE 165 years | URANUS 84 years | SATURN 29.5 years | JUPITER 12 years |

THE SOLAR SYSTEM TO SCALE

SUN · MERCURY · VENUS · EARTH · MARS · JUPITER · SATURN

One astronomical unit is 93 million miles (150 million kilometers), the average distance between the earth and the sun.

OUR PLACE IN THE UNIVERSE

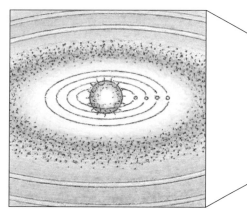

The sun at the center of our solar system is one of a few dozen stars in . . .

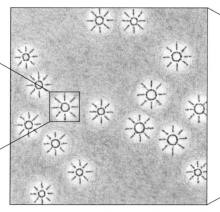

our local interstellar neighborhood, which forms a tiny part of . . .

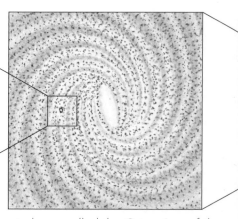

a spiral arm called the Orion Arm of the Milky Way galaxy, which is one of . . .

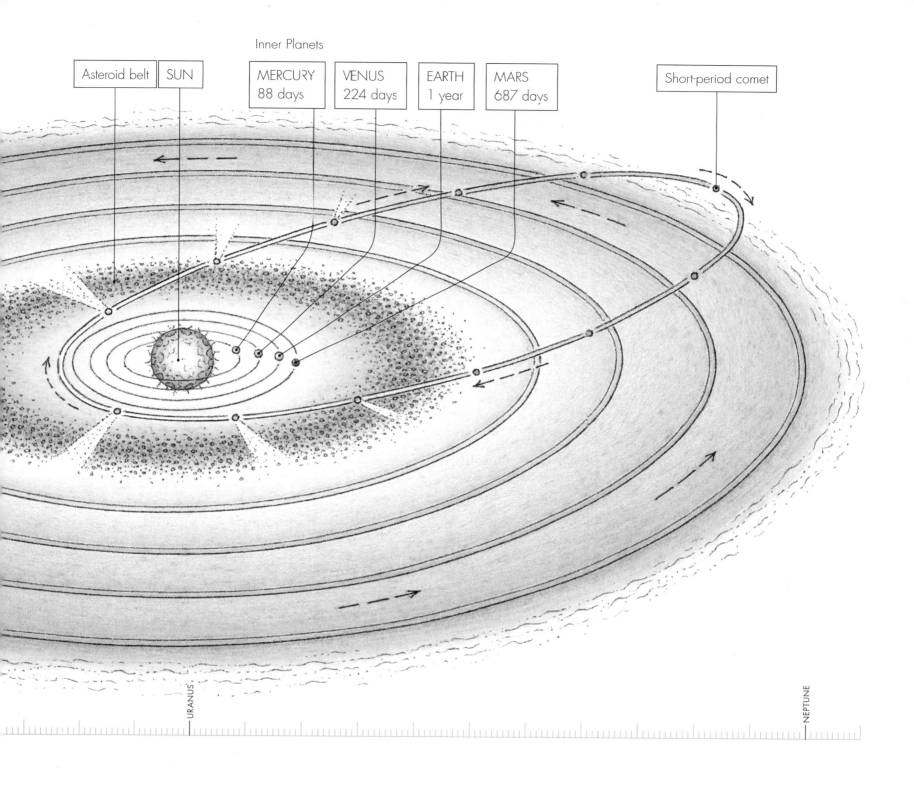

Inner Planets

Asteroid belt | SUN | MERCURY 88 days | VENUS 224 days | EARTH 1 year | MARS 687 days | Short-period comet

URANUS

NEPTUNE

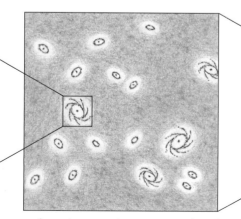

a few dozen galaxies in our local group of galaxies, which is part of . . .

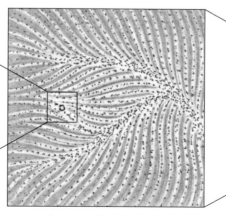

a supercluster called Laniakea, which contains about 100,000 galaxies . . .

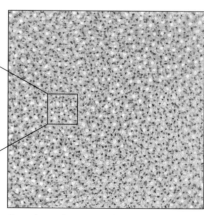

which is less than a millionth of the number of galaxies in the known universe.

During this time, we've discovered a huge amount about the solar system and about the universe beyond it. And we've truly come to realize just what a tiny part of that universe our solar system is. We now know that the sun is an ordinary, middle-aged, rather small star in one of the spiraling arms of the Milky Way. We know that there are between a hundred billion and a trillion other stars in the Milky Way and that the Milky Way itself is one of more than a hundred billion galaxies

in the universe as we can see it from Earth, each with untold numbers of stars in it. And from all that, we can make a guess at how many stars there are in the known universe altogether. You won't be surprised to hear it's an awful lot (one recent estimate is around 300,000,000,000,000,000,000,000).

We also know that the universe we can see is very large—about 93 billion light years across (a light year is the distance light travels in one year: about 6 trillion miles [9.5 trillion kilometers]). And we now know that it came into being in a very large explosion 13.8 billion years ago, and that it has been growing bigger ever since. But there's still plenty we don't know—including some really basic things, like what the universe is mostly made of. The stuff we can actually measure—the matter that makes up stars and planets (and us humans), and forms of energy like light and radio waves—only accounts for about one-twentieth of what we can figure out must really be there. Scientists refer to the other nineteen-twentieths as dark matter and dark energy, but they don't actually have a clue what either of those things is.

Something else we don't know is whether there's anybody else out there. The possibility there might be is the reason for *Voyager 1*'s Golden Record. It was never intended that any humans would ever listen to it once it left Earth. Instead, it's a message to the rest of the universe. The symbols on its cover are diagrams that show, without words, how to play it and where in the Milky Way it started out. If, just if, anything else ever comes across it and is intelligent enough to figure out what it is and how to listen to its sounds and decode its photographs, they might get an idea about us and some of the things that we on planet Earth thought were important at one brief moment in our history—things like the sound of crickets, a Chuck Berry song, a photo of the Taj Mahal, and a family portrait.

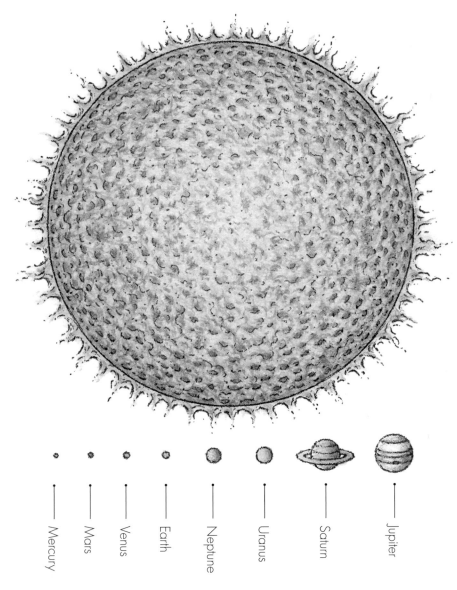

With a diameter of 865,000 miles (1,400,000 kilometers), the sun is by far the biggest object in the solar system. If it were shrunk to the size of an orange, the earth would be a poppy seed 26 feet (8 meters) away and Neptune a grape seed almost 800 feet (240 meters) down the street!

Mercury | Mars | Venus | Earth | Neptune | Uranus | Saturn | Jupiter

The Imperial Observatory in Beijing, China, was built before the invention of the telescope.

LOOKING AT THE SKY

These days, most of us don't have much trouble with the idea that our home is basically a minute ball of rock spinning around an ordinary star in an unimaginably huge universe. It hasn't always been like that. For a large part of history, people thought, quite understandably, that we humans must be at the center of things. After all, wasn't it obvious, just from looking, that the earth we lived on was fixed in place, and the sun and the moon and the stars all revolved around us, crossing the heavens every day or every night? Surely the earth was a flat disk of some kind, probably surrounded by sea, with the heavens forming a great bowl overhead through which these celestial objects all moved.

As people in the ancient world began to think more about geometry and math, some began to see problems with this model. The idea that the world was flat was one of the main sticking points. If that were true, why did ships traveling out to sea sink out of sight, with the top of the mast the last part to be seen, rather than just getting smaller until they were too small to be visible? That could make sense only if the surface of the earth was curved, not flat.

By around 300 BCE, astronomers in ancient Greece had figured out that the earth must be a globe, or sphere. About 250 BCE, one of them, Eratosthenes, even calculated how large it was, coming up with an answer impressively close to the right one—25,000 miles (40,000 kilometers) around the equator. A hundred years or so later, another, Hipparchus, estimated the distance of the moon from the earth and got that nearly right too; it's about 240,000 miles (390,000 kilometers).

Astronomers at that time also figured out that the sun was much farther away from the earth than the moon was, and was much bigger than either, although they did not realize just *how much* farther away and *how much* bigger. Still, some of them, most famously Aristarchus of Samos, even suggested that the earth might go around the sun instead of the other way around. People generally found that too hard to accept, so the idea that the earth was the center of the universe persisted.

Still, it wasn't easy understanding exactly how such a universe might work. One of the biggest headaches was explaining the movements of the so-called wandering stars. These were five stars that did not behave like the others. Instead of staying in a fixed pattern that rotated through the heavens in a regular way every night, they moved around, changing speeds and appearing in different parts of the pattern. Sometimes they weren't there at all. They were well known to astronomers everywhere and had different names in different parts of the world. To the Romans they were Mercurius, Venus, Mars, Jupiter, and Saturnus.

The best explanation for this puzzle, or at least the one that astronomers in Europe and the Islamic world stuck to for centuries, was proposed by a Greek-Egyptian astronomer named Ptolemy, who lived in the second century CE. According to his theory, the celestial objects were all fixed to transparent spheres, with smaller spheres rotating inside bigger ones that themselves rotated around the earth. Different objects were attached to different spheres, and some of the spheres themselves revolved at changing speeds.

Astronomers could figure out pretty well from this system what the future movements of the wandering stars would be. Since this was one of their main jobs, they were happy to keep using it, even though many of them could see that it had problems. The whole thing was very complicated, and it was hard to understand how it all actually operated up there in the sky. What made these invisible spheres revolve? Why did the speeds of

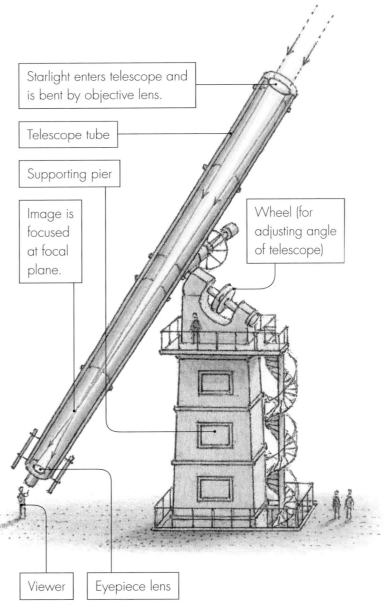

Starlight enters telescope and is bent by objective lens.

Telescope tube

Supporting pier

Image is focused at focal plane.

Wheel (for adjusting angle of telescope)

Viewer

Eyepiece lens

With a 40-inch- (1-meter-) diameter lens, the Yerkes Observatory refracting telescope, built in 1897, is a lot bigger than the telescopes Galileo used but works along exactly the same lines.

some of them change? How did they actually support the stars, the sun, and the moon?

Then, in 1543, Nicolaus Copernicus, a Polish scholar, published a book arguing that, while the moon did indeed revolve around the earth, the earth and the wandering stars actually revolved around the sun, as Aristarchus had suggested all those years before. Not only that, but the earth revolved around its own midline, or axis, once every 24 hours. This would explain why the stars and the sun appeared to rotate in the sky every 24 hours and could account for the strange movements of the wandering stars, or "planets" as they became known.

Some astronomers at the time were very taken with Copernicus's ideas. But others remained skeptical. Calculations based on his theory didn't quite agree with the exact movements of the planets as seen by sharp-eyed observers. That was because Copernicus thought that the planets moved in circles rather than in ellipses. This made it easier for people to stick to the old view, which was also the official view. And in most parts of the world at that time, it wasn't a good idea to disagree with the official view.

It might have stayed that way for a lot longer if the most important invention in the history of astronomy hadn't come along soon afterward. People had known for centuries that things looked different when seen through a lens—a curved piece of glass or clear crystal. A convex lens—one that bulges out in the center—acts as a magnifying glass, making close-up objects look bigger. A concave lens, thinner in the center than at the edge, makes far-off things look clearer. In the early 1600s, lens makers in the Netherlands discovered that if you put a convex lens at one end of a tube and a concave lens at the other and looked through the end with the concave lens, far-off objects appeared much bigger as well as clearer. They had invented the telescope.

News of this invention quickly spread across Europe. In June 1609 it reached Galileo Galilei, an Italian mathematician and inventor, who immediately started making telescopes of his own. Soon he managed to build one that could make a distant object appear 33 times as wide as it did to the naked eye. Using his invention, he saw things in the skies that no one had seen before. He discovered that Jupiter had tiny "stars" circling around it, he saw spots on the sun, and he saw that Venus gradually changed its appearance just like our moon, going from a crescent shape to a half circle, then a whole circle, then back again.

These things were hard to fit into the old view of the universe. If everything went around the earth, how come those "stars" went around Jupiter? And you could only really explain the way Venus behaved if it went around the sun, not the earth. All this pointed to Copernicus having been right. There were still problems—it was hard to explain why the fixed stars didn't seem to change their positions in the sky if the earth was moving, and many people found it impossible to believe that the huge, heavy earth could be hurtling through space.

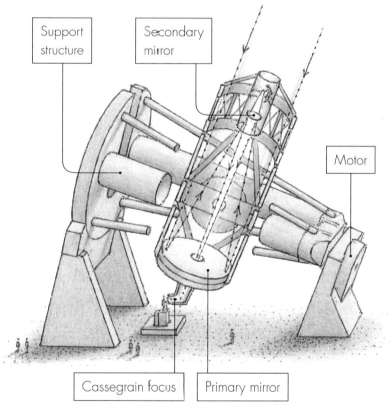

The Palomar Observatory's Hale telescope (1948) is a typical reflecting telescope, using a pair of curved mirrors as magnifiers. Light enters and bounces from the large primary mirror to the secondary mirror and then back through a hole in the primary mirror to a spot called the Cassegrain focus, where an enlarged image appears.

IT'S ALL DONE WITH MIRRORS

One of the world's most sophisticated telescopes is at the heart of the European Southern Observatory's Paranal facility, built on a specially flattened mountaintop high in the Chilean Andes. Four large reflecting telescopes, named after features of the sky in the local Mapuche language, are each powerful instruments in their own right. All four can also be combined to make an even more powerful kind of telescope called an interferometer.

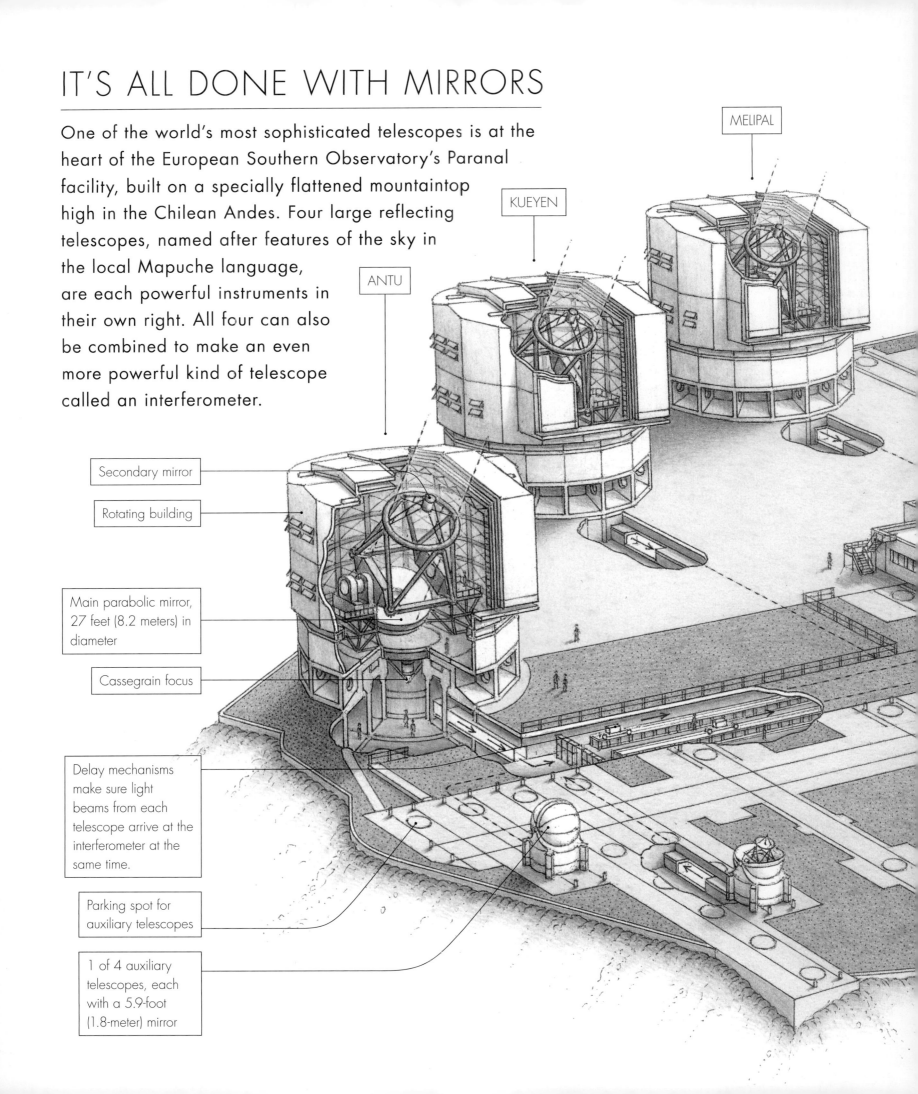

MELIPAL

KUEYEN

ANTU

Secondary mirror

Rotating building

Main parabolic mirror, 27 feet (8.2 meters) in diameter

Cassegrain focus

Delay mechanisms make sure light beams from each telescope arrive at the interferometer at the same time.

Parking spot for auxiliary telescopes

1 of 4 auxiliary telescopes, each with a 5.9-foot (1.8-meter) mirror

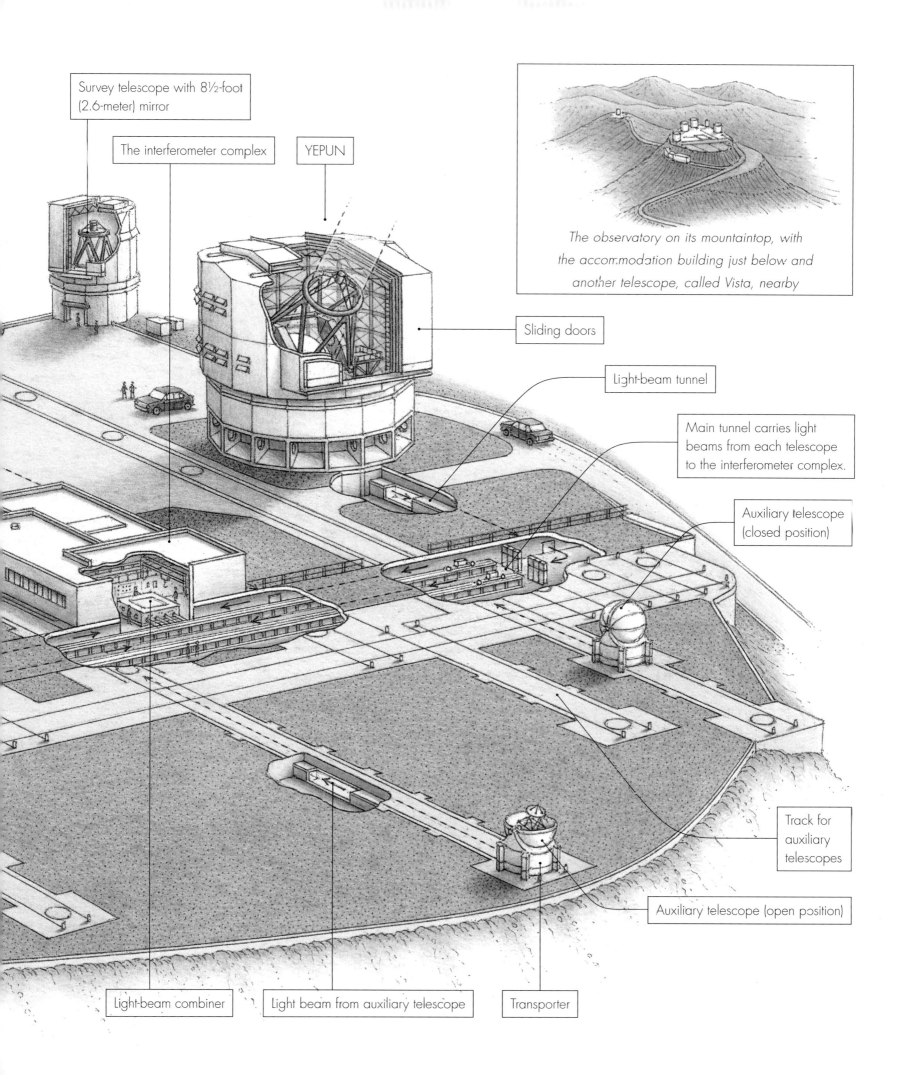

Survey telescope with 8½-foot (2.6-meter) mirror

The interferometer complex

YEPUN

The observatory on its mountaintop, with the accommodation building just below and another telescope, called Vista, nearby

Sliding doors

Light-beam tunnel

Main tunnel carries light beams from each telescope to the interferometer complex.

Auxiliary telescope (closed position)

Track for auxiliary telescopes

Auxiliary telescope (open position)

Light-beam combiner

Light beam from auxiliary telescope

Transporter

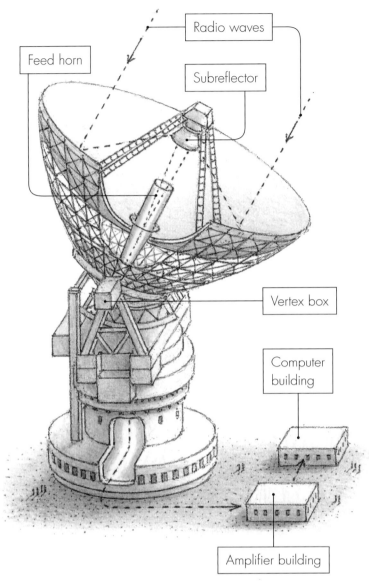

Radio waves

Feed horn

Subreflector

Vertex box

Computer building

Amplifier building

Radio telescopes such as the Yevpatoria RT-70 (1978) work in the same way as reflecting telescopes, but use radio waves instead of light. The waves are amplified before being analyzed by computer.

designed and built ever more powerful and accurate telescopes of both kinds. Lots of objects that had previously been too faint to be seen were discovered in the night sky, and far more detail could be made out in those that were already known. In 1781, William Herschel, using a reflecting telescope of his own design, discovered that something that had previously been thought to be a faint star was in fact a planet (though at first he thought it was a comet), which was later named Uranus. By watching the movements of Uranus very carefully, astronomers then figured out that there must be yet another planet out there. This led to the discovery of Neptune in 1846.

Refracting telescopes went on being used by professional astronomers until quite recently, but nowadays virtually all light-based astronomical telescopes are reflecting ones of various kinds—they're cheaper and easier to make. And now they've been joined by forms of telescopy that use other kinds of radiation, especially radio waves, but also X-rays and microwaves. Radio telescopy came about in the 1930s, when it was discovered (by accident) that metal antennas could pick up radio waves from space in the same way that mirrors and lenses pick up light waves. From here it was a short step to the invention of the radio telescope.

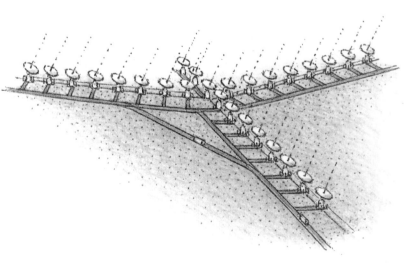

Acting as a single enormous radio telescope, the Very Large Array (1980) at Socorro, New Mexico, has 27 dishes arranged in a Y shape.

Although powerful bodies like the Catholic Church went on opposing Copernicus's view, more and more people in Europe began to accept it. Astronomy became a popular science and looking through telescopes a fashionable thing to do. At first the telescopes in use were all refracting ones that had glass lenses like Galileo's. Then, in 1668, a British scientist, Isaac Newton, knowing that a curved mirror behaved in a similar way to a glass lens, built the first reflecting telescope, which used mirrors instead of lenses.

In the years that followed, engineers and lens makers

Radio telescopes are much bigger than light-based ones — there's one at Arecibo in Puerto Rico that has a dish 1,000 feet (300 meters) across. Even this is dwarfed by modern array radio telescopes. Soon after radio astronomy was discovered, it was realized that the signals from a lot of separate small antennas spread across the ground could be combined, as if they formed part of one huge telescope. At first all the antennas making up one of these arrays were at one site, but as computers have grown more powerful, and it's now much easier to send information quickly across long distances, it's become possible to put antennas farther and farther apart. Some of today's array radio telescopes literally span continents.

People now use the same method of combining information from different receivers — it's called interferometry — with light telescopes, although on a much smaller scale. As a result, some of these telescopes can do amazing things. The European Southern Observatory's Very Large Telescope, at Paranal in Chile, would apparently be able to pick out the two separate headlights of a car on the moon.

But, however sophisticated they become, there will always be a limit to how accurate light-based telescopes on Earth can be. That's because of the earth's atmosphere, the layer of gases that surrounds the planet. The atmosphere is extremely important — it's the air that we breathe, and without it we couldn't survive. But to astronomers it's a bit of a problem. To reach a telescope on the ground, the light from space has to travel through the atmosphere, and this makes the light wobble, so that the view through the telescope is always a bit blurry. Astronomers have come up with clever ways of trying to overcome this, such as interferometry, but there's a limit to what they can do.

To get the clearest possible view, telescopes need to be above the earth's atmosphere, or rather telescopes that use light do (the atmosphere doesn't interfere with radio waves in the same way). And that's just where we've been putting them: in orbit hundreds of miles above the earth's surface.

Of course, before we could start putting telescopes in space, we had to learn how to get there in the first place. . . .

Launched in 1990, the Hubble Space Telescope is a reflecting telescope that orbits Earth 340 miles (550 km) up. Over the years, it has beamed hundreds of thousands of images back to Earth, including super-clear photos of some of the most distant objects in the universe.

GETTING INTO SPACE

There are stories of people flying, or trying to fly, from as far back as there are stories. Did a Chinese prisoner called Yuan Huangtou really float safely over the city walls of Yecheng in 559 CE when he was made to jump off a tower strapped to a giant kite? And in 1010 CE, did an English monk, Eilmer of Malmesbury, really use a pair of homemade wings to glide 650 feet (200 meters) through the air from a tower at Malmesbury Abbey before panicking and crash-landing, breaking both legs in the process? We'll never know for sure.

Luckily, the modern history of flying is more reliably recorded. It begins in France in the 1780s, when inventors designed balloons filled with hydrogen or hot air that were big enough to lift people off the ground. These were soon able to climb several thousand feet into the air and travel long distances, but no one seriously thought they could be used for exploring space. That remained something people only wrote about in stories. But some of these stories, most famously a novel published by Jules Verne in 1865 called *From the Earth to the Moon*, inspired the generation that launched the real space age. In the novel, three people in a space capsule are fired toward the moon from an enormous gun built in a hole in the ground in Florida.

We don't launch humans into space using a gun, but Verne was thinking along the right lines, as a Russian high-school math teacher named Konstantin Tsiolkovsky showed in his article "The Exploration of Outer Space by Means of Rocket Devices," published in 1903. In this article, Tsiolkovsky suggested that the solution to getting into space lay not with a gun but with something that worked in a similar way—a rocket.

In 1931, Auguste Piccard's balloon climbed to more than 50,000 feet (15,000 meters) — a world record then, but still a long way from the boundary with space.

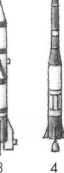

1   2   3   4

READY FOR TAKEOFF

Their shapes may differ, but all working space rockets since the late 1950s have been based on a similar multistage design, with fuel-filled rocket units discarded one after another as the fuel in them is used up. Before that, rockets had a single engine stage and were experimental prototypes or missiles.

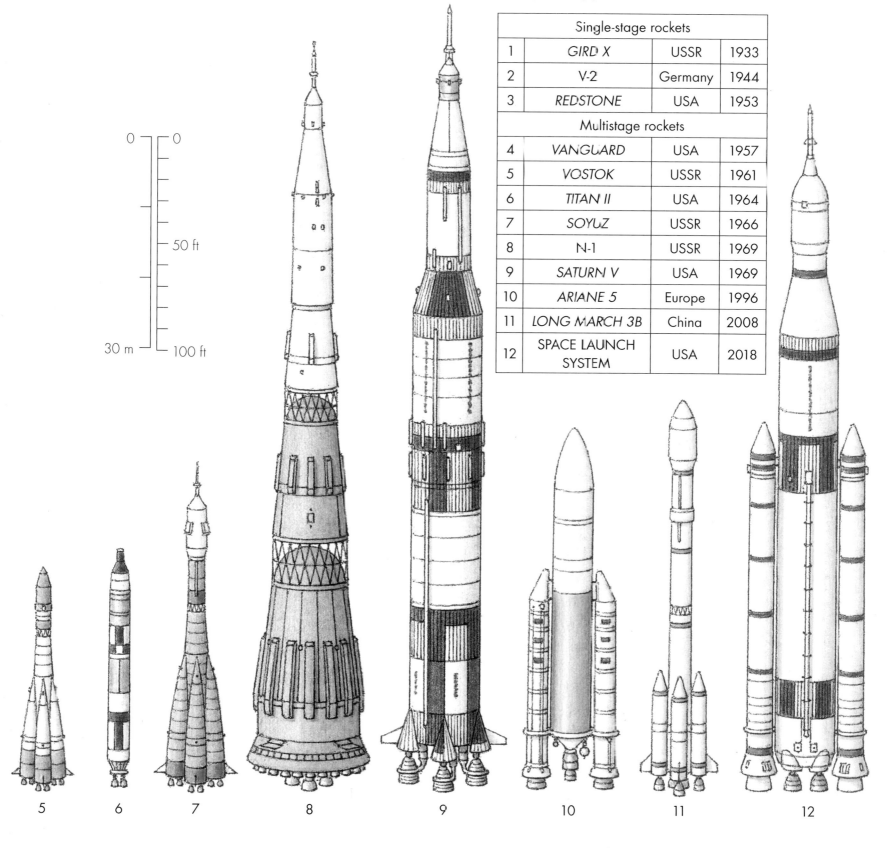

	Single-stage rockets		
1	*GIRD X*	USSR	1933
2	V-2	Germany	1944
3	*REDSTONE*	USA	1953
	Multistage rockets		
4	*VANGUARD*	USA	1957
5	*VOSTOK*	USSR	1961
6	*TITAN II*	USA	1964
7	*SOYUZ*	USSR	1966
8	N-1	USSR	1969
9	*SATURN V*	USA	1969
10	*ARIANE 5*	Europe	1996
11	*LONG MARCH 3B*	China	2008
12	SPACE LAUNCH SYSTEM	USA	2018

5   6   7   8   9   10   11   12

BIG ROCKETS NEED TALL BUILDINGS

Saturn V remains the tallest and most powerful rocket ever launched. The three main stages were built in different places (two in California and one in New Orleans) and assembled at the Kennedy Space Center in Florida in the Vertical (now "Vehicle") Assembly Building. At 525 feet (160 meters), this is still the tallest single-story building in the world, tall enough for clouds to form inside.

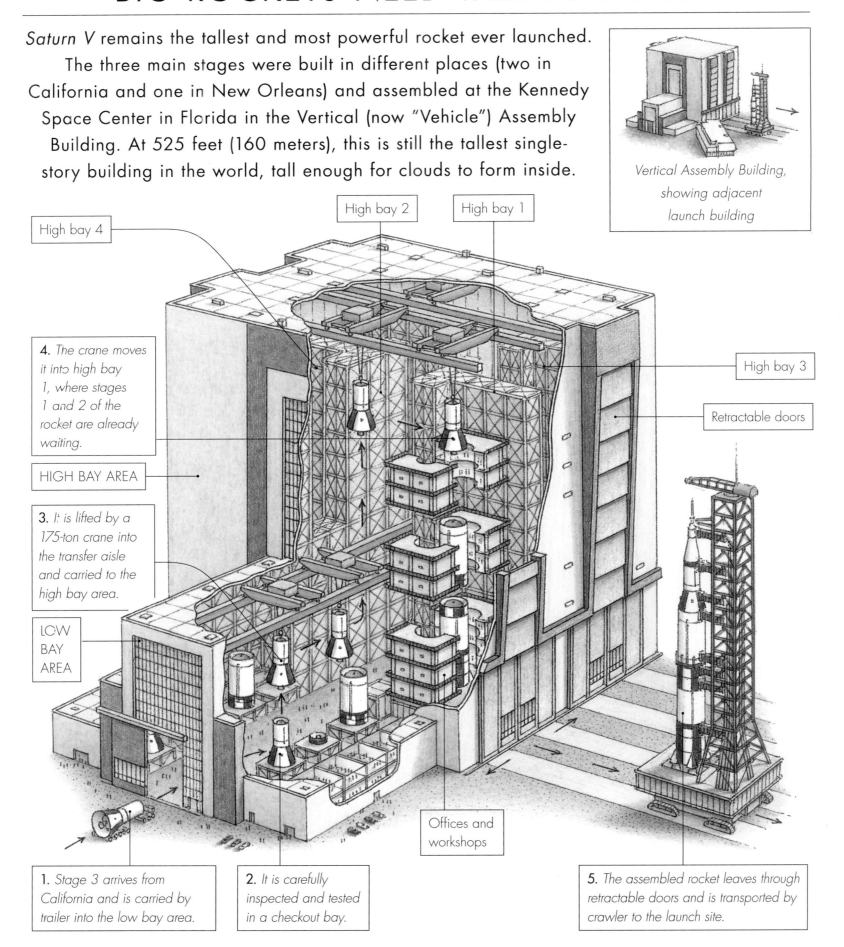

Vertical Assembly Building, showing adjacent launch building

High bay 4

High bay 2

High bay 1

High bay 3

Retractable doors

4. *The crane moves it into high bay 1, where stages 1 and 2 of the rocket are already waiting.*

HIGH BAY AREA

3. *It is lifted by a 175-ton crane into the transfer aisle and carried to the high bay area.*

LOW BAY AREA

Offices and workshops

1. *Stage 3 arrives from California and is carried by trailer into the low bay area.*

2. *It is carefully inspected and tested in a checkout bay.*

5. *The assembled rocket leaves through retractable doors and is transported by crawler to the launch site.*

People had known about guns and rockets for a long time. Both are based on gunpowder, or "black powder," a Chinese invention. When black powder burns, it makes a large amount of gas very quickly. If this happens in a small space, it creates a lot of pressure. If the space is the chamber of a gun, with a tube or barrel coming out of it containing a bullet, the pressure from the gas should force the bullet out of the barrel—it's like blowing a spitball out of a straw. If the space where the powder burns is the fuel compartment of a rocket, with a hole or nozzle at one end, then the gas will come rushing out of the hole. The effect of that is to push the rocket in the opposite direction. This is one of the consequences of the laws of motion set out by Isaac Newton (of the reflecting telescope) in 1687. You can try it out by standing on a skateboard or wearing roller skates and throwing a ball away from you; you'll immediately roll in the opposite direction. The ball is like the gas, and you are the rocket.

There's one big, and very important, difference between a gun and a rocket. In a gun, the force of the gas all goes into speeding up the bullet before it's left the gun. Once the bullet has come out of the barrel, the gas can't provide any more force to help it keep going if other forces are working against it. For a bullet, or anything else, heading away from the earth into space, there are two very important forces doing just that. These are the earth's gravity, which pulls objects back down to Earth, and resistance from the earth's atmosphere, which slows objects moving through it.

But a rocket carries its own fuel, which can continue to burn and provide force to help the rocket overcome both gravity and air resistance as it continues its flight. (So it's actually more like you standing on a skateboard with a bucket of balls, which you keep throwing away from you, in which case your skateboard will keep rolling along in the opposite direction.)

Tsiolkovsky explained all this in his article. He also showed how much fuel a rocket would need to be able to get into space—it depended on how heavy the rocket was, but in any event it was a lot. And he suggested that

there were liquid fuels that might be better than solid ones like black powder, as they could provide more force for the same weight.

At first, Tsiolkovsky's article was little known outside Russia, but in other parts of the world, other people, also often inspired by Jules Verne's novels, were thinking along the same lines. Societies for the study and promotion of rocket travel sprang up in several countries, and people began to build and try out small experimental rockets, something that Tsiolkovsky never did. One of them was an American named Robert Goddard. Like many rocket pioneers, Goddard found it hard to get other people, especially in governments and universities, to take his ideas seriously. He worked mostly alone, often with little money. In 1926, he successfully launched the world's first liquid-fuel rocket, using a specially shaped nozzle called a de Laval nozzle. His first rocket went only 41 feet (12.5 meters) into the air, but it showed what could be done. Goddard, like Tsiolkovsky, thought that the way into space was via multistage rockets, with several fuel compartments that would detach from the rocket once the fuel in them was used up, thereby keeping the weight of the rocket as low as possible.

The first country to take rocket science seriously was the Soviet Union (the country Russia was part of at the time). In 1931, the government there set up a Group for the Study of Reactive Motion, or GIRD, headed by the scientist Sergei Korolev. Later in the 1930s, another government became very interested in rockets—that of Nazi Germany. However, rockets weren't being thought of as a way of traveling into space, but rather as long-distance weapons.

World War II broke out in 1939, and the Nazi government stepped up its rocket research, under the direction of the scientist Wernher von Braun. Using forced labor, his team produced the V-2 rocket missile, also known as the A-4 or *Aggregat-4*, which carried an explosive warhead and was used as a weapon during the war. It could travel at over 3,000 mph (5,000 kph) and reach an altitude of more than 125 miles (200 kilometers),

THE WORLD'S BUSIEST ROCKET

Rockets of the Soyuz family are true workhorses. More than 1,500 have been launched since the original was introduced in 1966, far more than any other kind of rocket. One of their many jobs is carrying astronauts to the International Space Station (ISS).

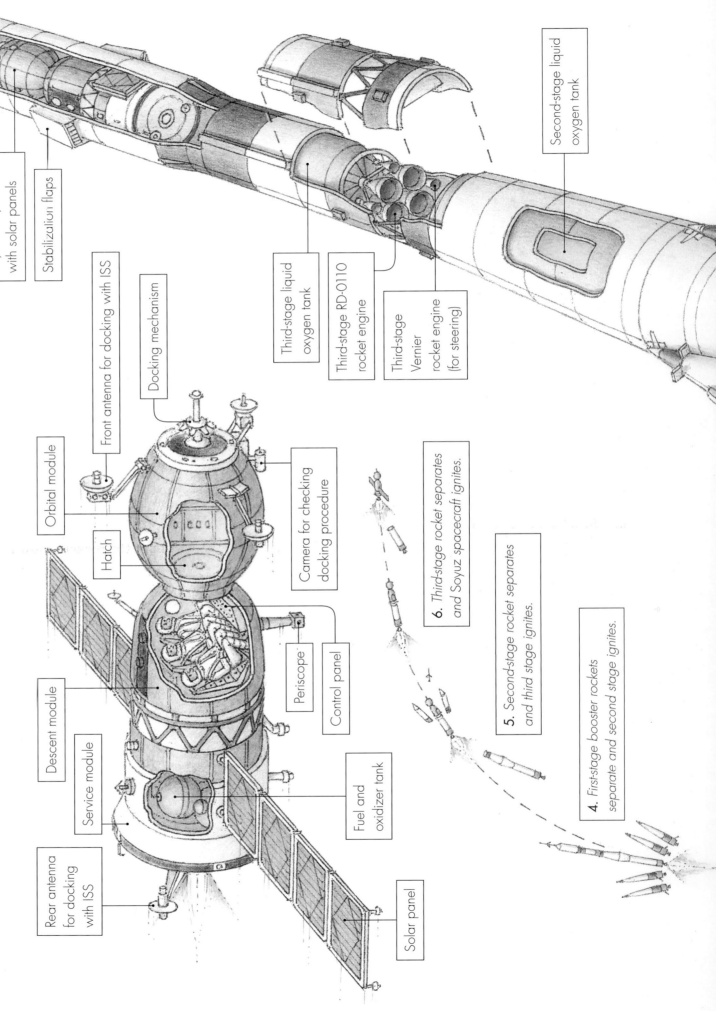

Rocket escape system

Soyuz-TM spacecraft with solar panels

Stabilization flaps

Second-stage liquid oxygen tank

Third-stage liquid oxygen tank

Third-stage RD-0110 rocket engine

Third-stage Vernier rocket engine (for steering)

Front antenna for docking with ISS

Docking mechanism

Orbital module

Hatch

Camera for checking docking procedure

Descent module

Periscope

Control panel

Service module

Fuel and oxidizer tank

Rear antenna for docking with ISS

Solar panel

6. Third-stage rocket separates and Soyuz spacecraft ignites.

5. Second-stage rocket separates and third stage ignites.

4. First-stage booster rockets separate and second stage ignites.

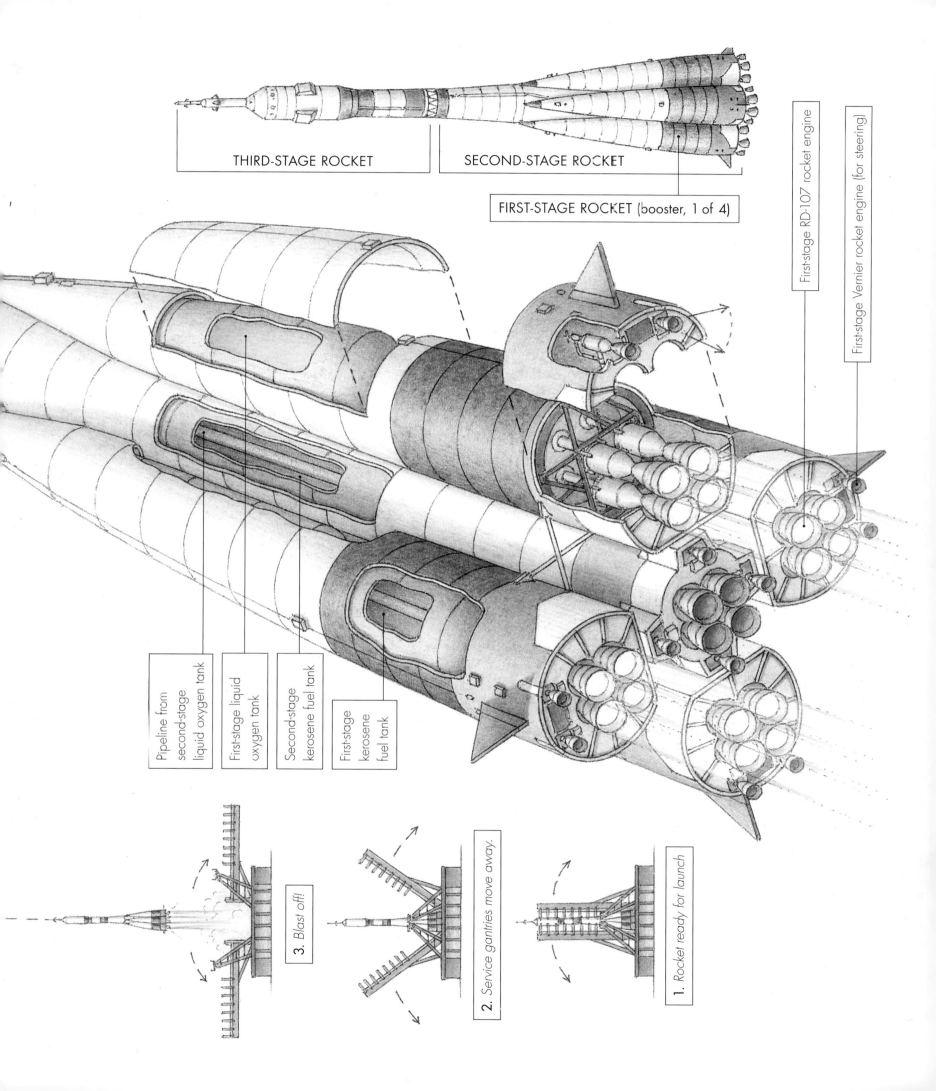

THIRD-STAGE ROCKET

SECOND-STAGE ROCKET

FIRST-STAGE ROCKET (booster, 1 of 4)

First-stage RD-107 rocket engine

First-stage Vernier rocket engine (for steering)

Pipeline from second-stage liquid oxygen tank

First-stage liquid oxygen tank

Second-stage kerosene fuel tank

First-stage kerosene fuel tank

3. Blast off!

2. Service gantries move away.

1. Rocket ready for launch

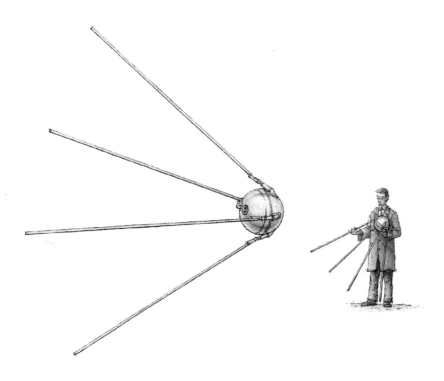

The world's first artificial satellite, Sputnik 1, circled Earth 1,440 times between October 1957 and January 1958.

lasted a year and a half). Scientists from all over the world would work together on scientific projects studying the earth and its atmosphere. In 1955 the United States and the Soviet Union each announced that they would launch an artificial satellite as part of their contribution to the year. The real race into space (not counting missiles) was on.

In the end, it was the Soviet Union that won this first challenge. On October 4, 1957, a modified R-7 rocket was launched from a Soviet missile base at Tyuratam, in what is now Kazakhstan. Instead of a warhead, the rocket carried an artificial satellite — a shiny sphere 23 inches (58 centimeters) across and weighing 184 pounds (84 kilograms). The satellite, named *Sputnik 1*, didn't contain very much, just a couple of simple sensors and a short-wave radio transmitter, but it was a global sensation. For three months it circled the earth, traveling at 18,000 mph (29,000 kph) and making a complete revolution every 96 minutes. The batteries in its radio transmitters lasted 22 days, during which its *beep-beep-beep* was picked up by amateur radio operators worldwide.

In the United States, many people were horrified that the Soviet Union had beaten them. The program to launch an American satellite was rushed forward. The first attempt, on December 6, 1957, failed seconds after takeoff, but success came at the end of January, when a *Juno 1* rocket, based on the *Redstone* missile, put the satellite *Explorer 1* into orbit.

The next great step, as far as most people were concerned, was to get a human into space. The United States and the Soviet Union both set to work on this goal. They had already been experimenting by sending various animals up in rockets, but many of these had died. Then on April 12, 1961, the Soviet Union stunned the world once more when cosmonaut Yuri Gagarin made a complete orbit of the earth, taking 108 minutes, in a spacecraft called *Vostok 1*. The Soviet Union had beaten the United States again. Three weeks later, the American Alan Shepard became the second person in space, although his flight lasted only 15 minutes and he did not complete an orbit.

thus becoming the first man-made object to reach space (nowadays taken as starting at 62 miles [100 kilometers] above the earth's surface).

When the war ended in 1945, the United States and the Soviet Union both raced to get their hands on German rocket secrets — and rocket scientists. Although the two countries had been allies during the war, they soon became rivals, each deeply suspicious of the other. A period known as the Cold War began, and rocket scientists were put to work developing ever larger and more powerful rocket missiles. Wernher von Braun had surrendered to the United States in 1945 and was made the head of the US team that turned the V-2 into the *Redstone* rocket. In the Soviet Union, rocket engineers led by Sergei Korolev concentrated on their own designs, coming up with the R series.

Although most of their work was in weapons systems, scientists in both countries held on to the idea that rockets could also be used to explore space and for other peaceful purposes. In the 1950s came a chance to do this. The period from July 1, 1957, to December 31, 1958, was declared the International Geophysical Year (though it

It was becoming hard for American politicians to explain why the country was always behind. In 1962, President John F. Kennedy persuaded the government to put a lot more money into the US space program. In September he made a speech in Houston, Texas, in which he said, "We choose to go to the moon," promising that an American astronaut would land there before 1970.

Although they did not state it publicly, the Soviet Union also began planning to put a man on the moon. For the next few years both countries made huge progress with manned spaceflights, although there were many setbacks and some terrible accidents.

At first the Soviet Union kept its lead, but in 1966 Sergei Korolev died, dealing a major blow to the Soviet space program. By 1968, the United States was clearly ahead. In December, the US spacecraft *Apollo 8* carried three astronauts around the moon and back—the first time any humans had left the immediate vicinity of Earth. Two more trial spaceflights, *Apollo*s 9 and 10, followed. Then, on July 16, 1969, *Apollo 11* was launched, carrying three astronauts: Buzz Aldrin, Neil Armstrong, and Michael Collins. Four days later, following a 240,000-mile (386,000-kilometer) journey from Earth and thirteen orbits of the moon, the lunar module *Eagle* separated from the command module *Columbia* and began to descend, landing safely on the moon two and a half hours later in an area known as the Sea of Tranquillity. Six and a half hours after that, the module's hatch was opened; Neil Armstrong emerged (it was a tight squeeze), climbed down a nine-rung ladder, and stepped onto the moon's surface. President Kennedy's promise had been honored.

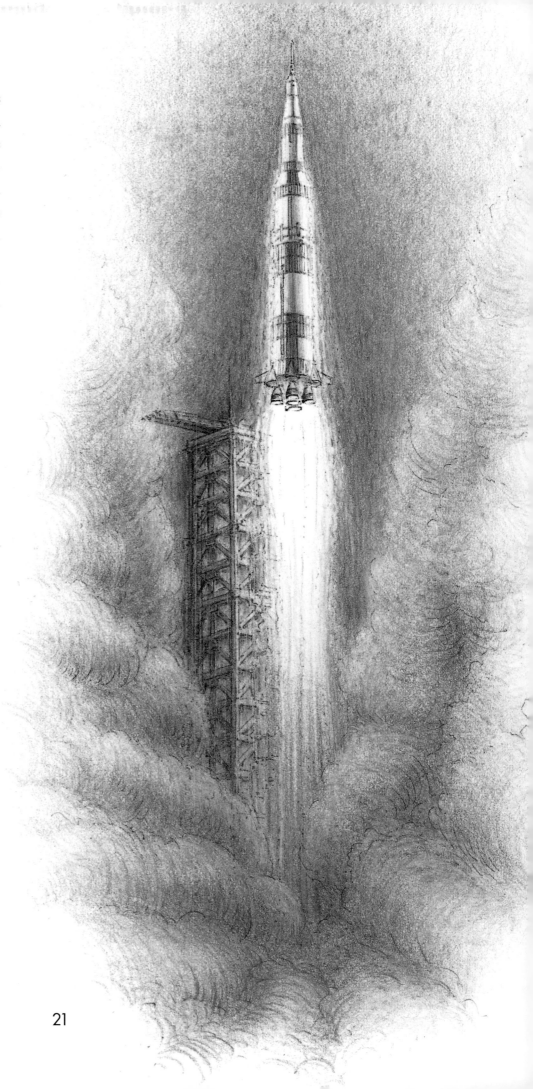

BLASTOFF: A Saturn V rocket takes off carrying the Apollo 11 spacecraft on its way to the moon.

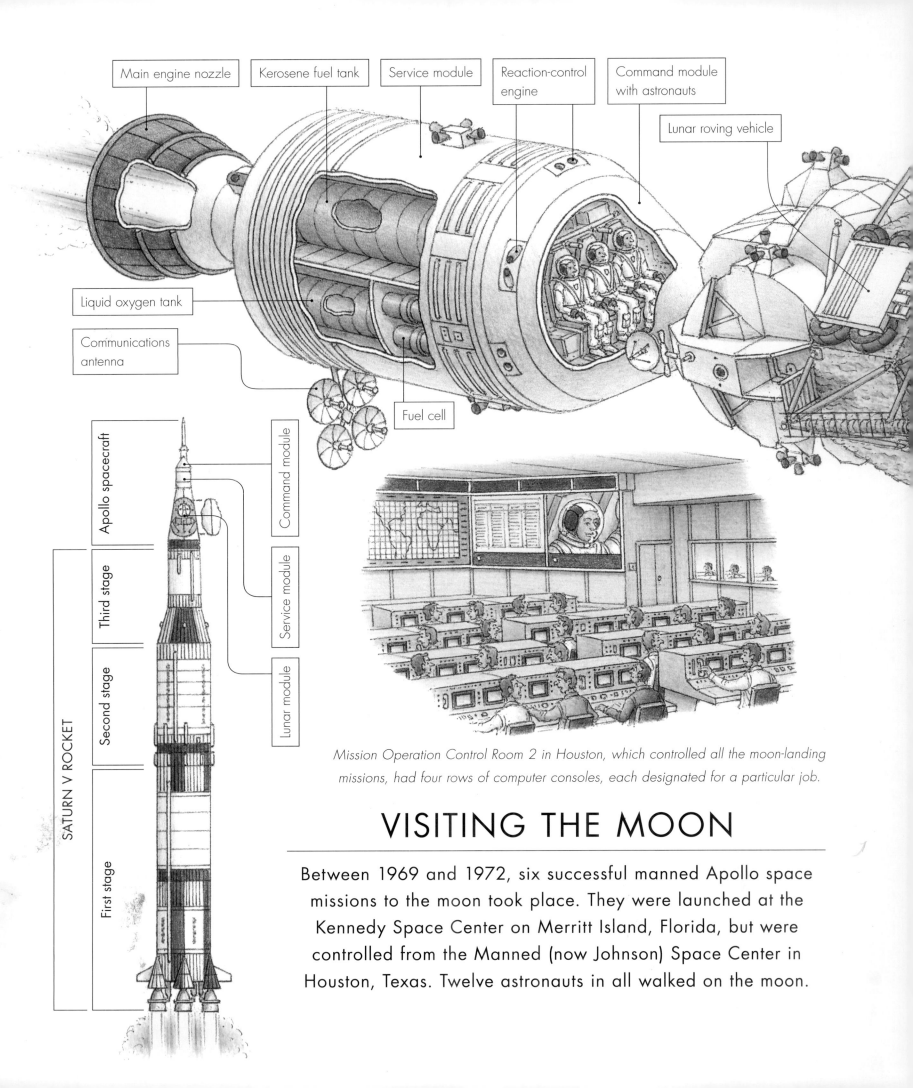

Main engine nozzle

Kerosene fuel tank

Service module

Reaction-control engine

Command module with astronauts

Lunar roving vehicle

Liquid oxygen tank

Communications antenna

Fuel cell

Apollo spacecraft

Third stage

Second stage

First stage

SATURN V ROCKET

Command module

Service module

Lunar module

Mission Operation Control Room 2 in Houston, which controlled all the moon-landing missions, had four rows of computer consoles, each designated for a particular job.

VISITING THE MOON

Between 1969 and 1972, six successful manned Apollo space missions to the moon took place. They were launched at the Kennedy Space Center on Merritt Island, Florida, but were controlled from the Manned (now Johnson) Space Center in Houston, Texas. Twelve astronauts in all walked on the moon.

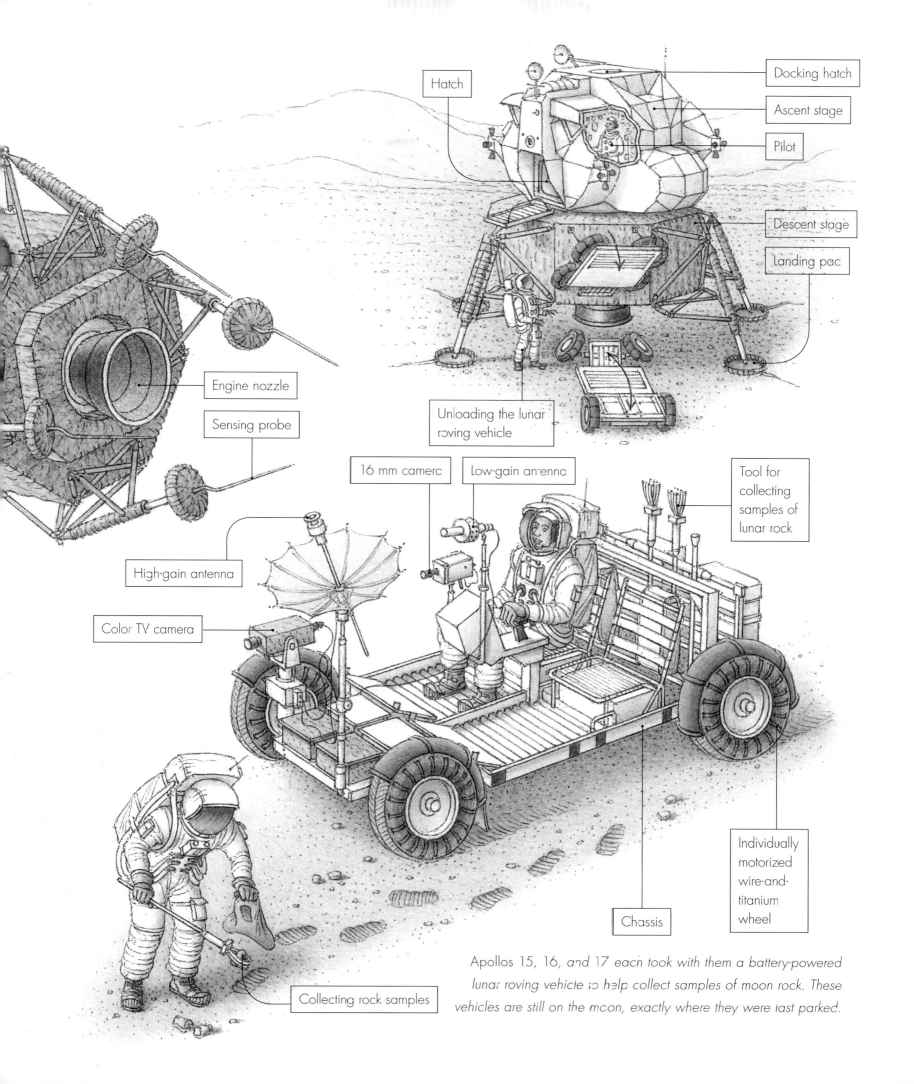

Hatch

Docking hatch

Ascent stage

Pilot

Descent stage

Landing pad

Engine nozzle

Sensing probe

Unloading the lunar roving vehicle

16 mm camera

Low-gain antenna

Tool for collecting samples of lunar rock

High-gain antenna

Color TV camera

Chassis

Individually motorized wire-and-titanium wheel

Collecting rock samples

Apollos 15, 16, and 17 each took with them a battery-powered lunar roving vehicle to help collect samples of moon rock. These vehicles are still on the moon, exactly where they were last parked.

Like other spacecraft, the Space Shuttle generated a vast amount of heat when it reentered Earth's atmosphere.

COMING BACK TO EARTH

Getting humans into space, let alone to the moon, is an incredible achievement. But so is getting them safely back. Each is difficult, and dangerous, in its own way. At takeoff, there's the ever-present risk of an explosion. As Tsiolkovsky showed, for a rocket to get into space, it has to carry a huge amount of fuel, since it needs to generate enough energy to overcome both the force of the earth's gravity pulling it back and resistance from the earth's atmosphere impeding its forward motion. If anything goes wrong in the early stages of a rocket's

voyage, the chances of all that fuel going up in flames are pretty high.

Air resistance doesn't just slow a speeding rocket down; it also heats it up. Below the speed of sound (around 770 mph [1,200 kph] in the air), the main reason for heat generation is friction between the outside of the rocket and gas molecules in the air. The faster the rocket goes and the thicker the atmosphere, the more friction there is. And the more friction there is, the hotter the rocket gets. At very high speeds something else can happen as well. By pushing hard against the air immediately in front of it, a rocket can heat up this air enormously, creating a super-hot shock wave, which may then wash over the rocket, making it far hotter than friction alone would.

Rockets on takeoff need protection from heat created by friction, but they are not going fast enough to generate major shock waves. As they climb, they go faster, but at the same time the atmosphere gets thinner. It quite quickly becomes too thin for either shock waves or friction to be a major problem. Above the atmosphere, there is no air resistance, and space vehicles can hurtle along at incredible speeds without getting heated up at all.

For vehicles coming back to Earth, it's a different story. They are almost always moving very fast at about 17,500 mph (28,000 kph). This is fast enough to cause a shock wave even in the thin air of the upper part of the atmosphere. The temperature created is so high that most objects would simply burn up (that's what shooting stars are: rocks or rocky particles from space burning up as they enter the atmosphere).

Once a space vehicle has survived the perils of reentry, it still has to be brought safely back down to Earth. Left to its own devices, it would fall through the earth's atmosphere until it reached a steady speed, known as its terminal speed or terminal velocity. It would then keep going at that speed until it crashed into the ground. The terminal velocity of a spaceship is around 185 mph (300 kph). No human could survive hitting the ground that fast.

So engineers trying to bring astronauts safely back down to Earth have two problems to solve: how to keep their vehicle from burning up on reentry, and how to slow down its fall so that it does not crash into the ground at a fatal speed.

They found a straightforward answer to the second problem: parachutes, which people had been using to jump off things and out of balloons and airplanes for many years. The first problem was more difficult. For a long time, rocket designers thought that spaceships

should be pointed and streamlined to keep them from heating up too much on reentry into the atmosphere. Then, in the 1950s, two scientists realized that in fact just the opposite was the case, and the blunter the front of the vehicle, the better. The blunt end slows the vehicle down quickly, and creates a cushion of air in front of it that pushes the thermal shock wave away from the vehicle, keeping its surface from getting as hot as it otherwise would.

It still gets pretty hot, though—about 2,700°F (1,500°C). Obviously, if the astronauts on board are going to survive, the inside of the space vehicle has to stay a lot cooler than that. The solution, developed in the early days of space travel, was something called an ablative heat shield. This is an outer layer on the spacecraft made of a substance that mostly gets used up during reentry into the atmosphere. The substance undergoes a chemical change in the intense heat, producing large amounts of gas that blow away from the spacecraft, carrying a lot of the heat with it. Under this are layers of more usual insulation that keep the remaining heat from entering the spacecraft.

This was the way that all the early astronauts returned from space and is how all astronauts today come back—in a small capsule with a rounded or blunt end, protected by an ablative heat shield, with parachutes that come into operation when the capsule is still a few miles above the earth's surface. Even with parachutes, the capsule will still come down fast enough to cause quite a bump on landing, enough to risk injuring anyone inside. To get around this, American space capsules have always landed out at sea, where the water acts as a cushion—that's why these landings are called splashdowns. This method works well, but it makes picking up returning space travelers a complicated business, needing ships and reconnaissance aircraft.

Russian and now Chinese space capsules have instead usually come down on land. In the very early days of the Soviet space program, the astronauts bailed out of the capsule a few miles up, landing safely with their own

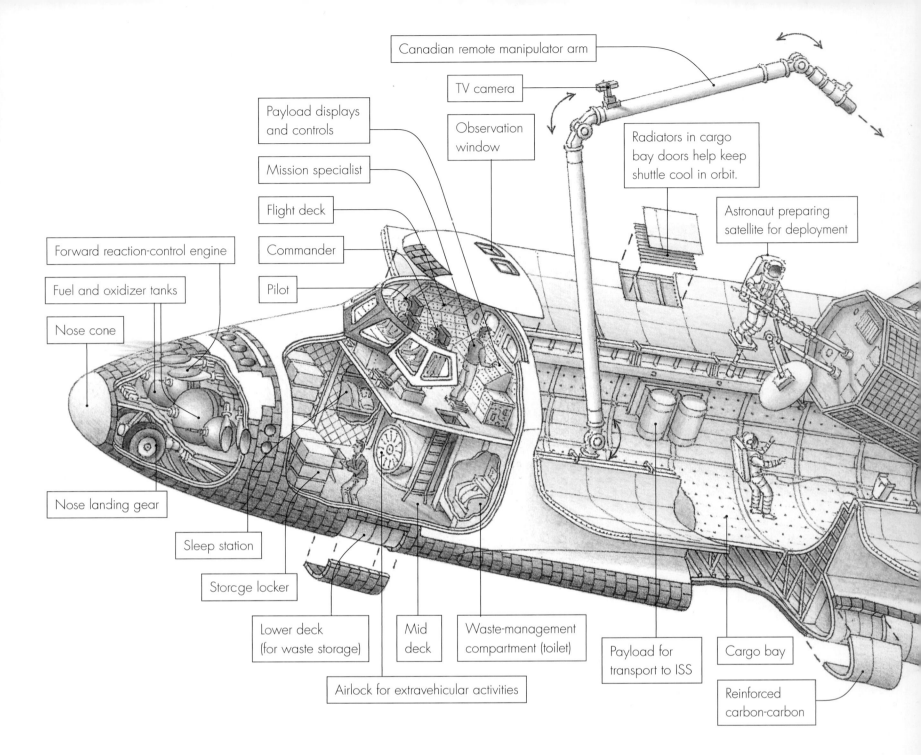

Canadian remote manipulator arm

TV camera

Observation window

Radiators in cargo bay doors help keep shuttle cool in orbit.

Payload displays and controls

Astronaut preparing satellite for deployment

Mission specialist

Flight deck

Commander

Forward reaction-control engine

Pilot

Fuel and oxidizer tanks

Nose cone

Nose landing gear

Sleep station

Storage locker

Lower deck (for waste storage)

Mid deck

Waste-management compartment (toilet)

Payload for transport to ISS

Cargo bay

Reinforced carbon-carbon

Airlock for extravehicular activities

A PLANE IN SPACE

The Space Shuttles were space vehicles that took off like any other rocket but could land on a runway like a normal airplane. They ferried crew and materials to and from the International Space Station (ISS) and launched space probes and satellites, as well as carrying out servicing missions to satellites already in orbit. Among their cargoes were the probes *Galileo*, which traveled to Jupiter, and *Magellan*, which mapped the surface of Venus. The Hubble Space Telescope was also launched from a shuttle and was visited by five servicing missions, the last of which took place in 2009.

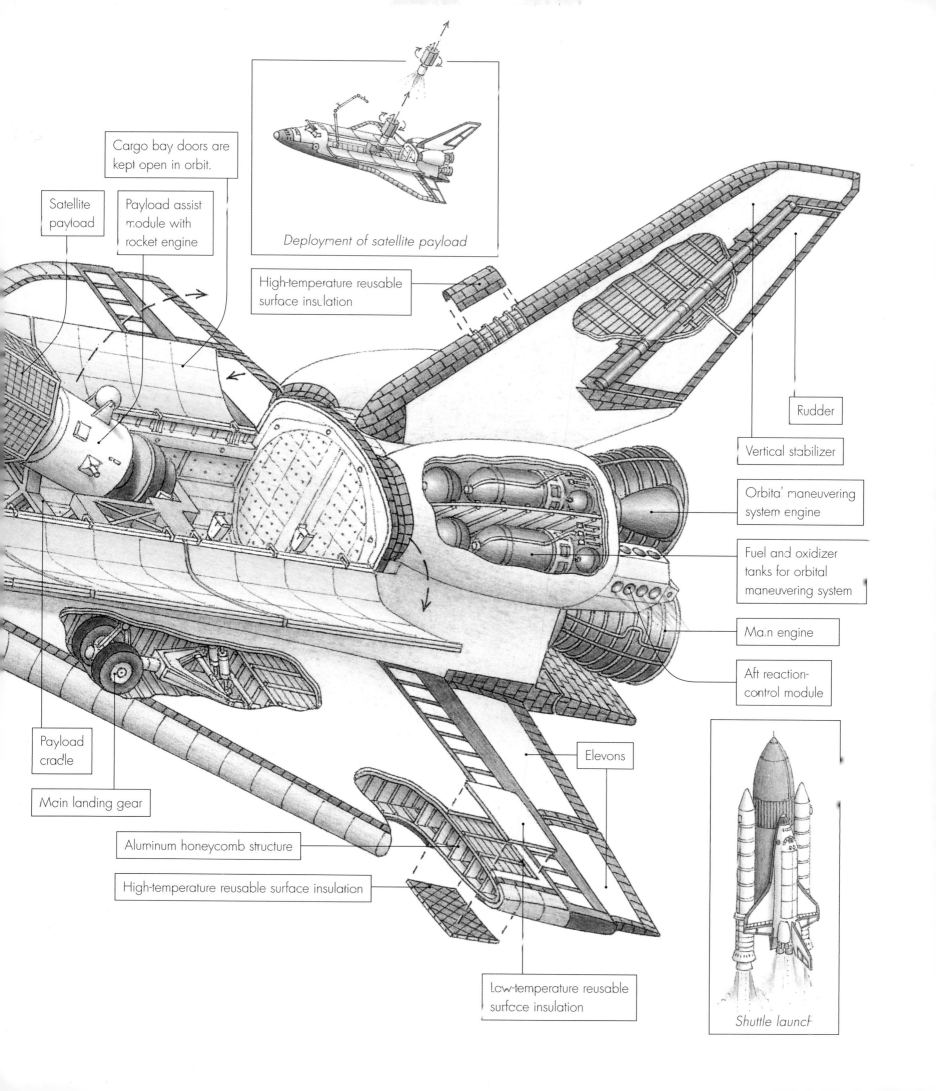

Cargo bay doors are kept open in orbit.

Satellite payload

Payload assist module with rocket engine

High-temperature reusable surface insulation

Deployment of satellite payload

Rudder

Vertical stabilizer

Orbital maneuvering system engine

Fuel and oxidizer tanks for orbital maneuvering system

Main engine

Aft reaction-control module

Payload cradle

Main landing gear

Elevons

Aluminum honeycomb structure

High-temperature reusable surface insulation

Low-temperature reusable surface insulation

Shuttle launch

Splashdown!

personal parachutes, leaving the capsule to come down to Earth with a clunk and a couple of bounces. Nowadays, small retro-rockets fixed to the capsule are fired a second before landing. These act as brakes, slowing down the very last bit of the descent so that there should be no more than a slight jolt on landing.

This way of getting into space and back again has been tried and tested and is very successful. The problem is that it's also very wasteful and expensive. Each rocket and each spacecraft is used just once. The only part that comes back to Earth in one piece is the reentry capsule, and that is never used again.

From the very start, engineers have tried to come up with space vehicles that could be used more than once. An obvious answer was some kind of space plane — something that took off and landed like an airplane but could go into space. In fact, it has proven surprisingly difficult to design a vehicle that can do this. In the United States in the early 1960s, quite a lot of progress was made developing a space plane called the *Dyna-Soar*, but the project was canceled as it was costing a huge amount of money and the government decided to concentrate on getting to the moon instead.

In 1969, NASA started another ambitious program to develop a reusable spacecraft. The result of this, the Space Shuttle, was launched in 1981. The five shuttles that went into service carried out 135 space missions between them before the last one, the *Atlantis*, was retired in July 2011. The Space Shuttle was never entirely reusable — its huge 154-foot- (47-meter-) long main fuel tank was jettisoned soon after takeoff to disintegrate in the upper atmosphere — but it was a remarkable piece of technology. It had a revolutionary heat-protection system, it could carry seven astronauts as well as larger cargo loads than any other space vehicle in one trip, and it landed on a runway like a normal aircraft. However, it never really succeeded in its main aim, which was to make travel into space cheap and reliable. The shuttles proved extremely expensive to run — much more expensive than conventional disposable rockets — and two of them suffered terrible accidents: the *Challenger* on takeoff in 1986 and the *Columbia* on reentry in 2003.

The Space Shuttles may be retired, but people have not given up on the idea of reusable space vehicles. A number of different ones have been proposed or are being developed, mostly by private companies, some for space tourism and some as part of ambitious longer-term plans to establish settlements on the moon or to get humans to Mars.

FIVE WAYS TO LAUNCH A SPACE PLANE

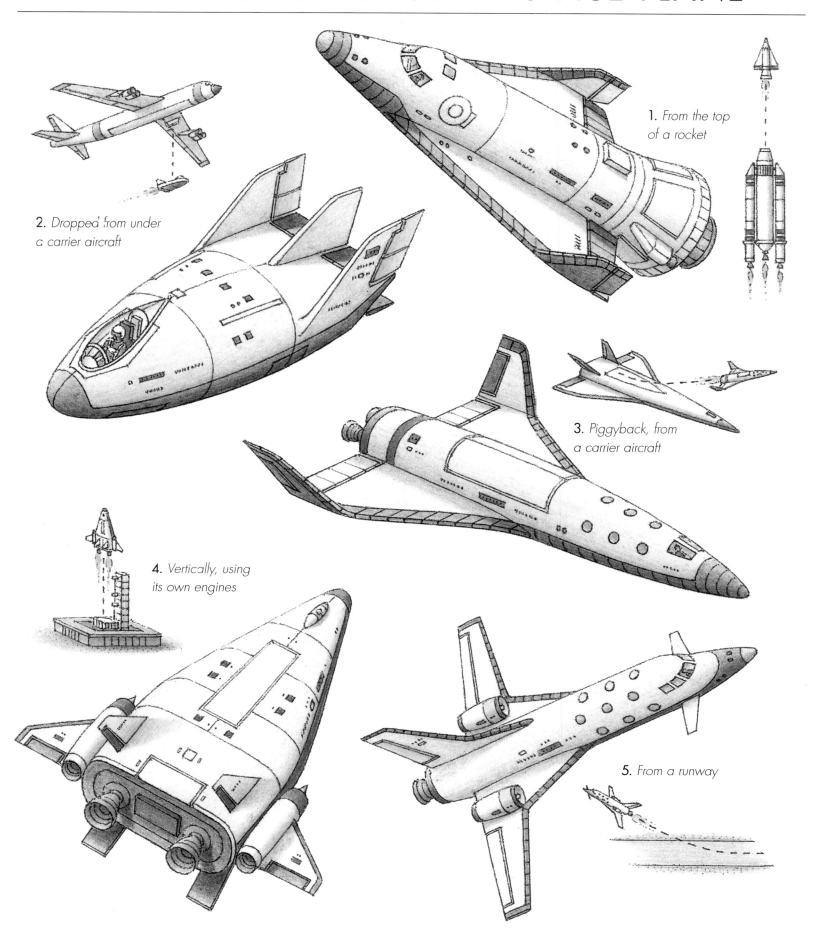

1. *From the top of a rocket*

2. *Dropped from under a carrier aircraft*

3. *Piggyback, from a carrier aircraft*

4. *Vertically, using its own engines*

5. *From a runway*

Astronauts make repairs to the International Space Station as it orbits Earth.

SURVIVING IN SPACE

There's a lot about living on the earth's surface that we take for granted. Gravity, for a start. It gives us weight. It makes us fall if there isn't something holding us up. It makes it harder to lift heavy things than light things, and more exhausting to climb stairs than to walk on a flat surface. It's not visible, but it operates on us, and everything around us, all the time.

Then there's the air that we breathe — the atmosphere that holds back rockets and irritates astronomers by blurring their view of the stars. We can't see that either, and we certainly take it for granted, but without it we'd very quickly die. It's a mixture of gases, about one-fifth oxygen and almost all the rest nitrogen, with very small amounts of other gases, mainly argon and carbon dioxide. There's water vapor in it too — that's what makes up clouds. Like almost all other living creatures, we need oxygen to survive. Carbon dioxide is the gas that we and other living things produce when we respire. In large quantities, it's poisonous to animals such as humans, but plants need it to grow. Nitrogen and argon are nonpoisonous.

THE ULTIMATE OUTFIT

Since these suits cost millions of dollars each, there are only a handful in the world!

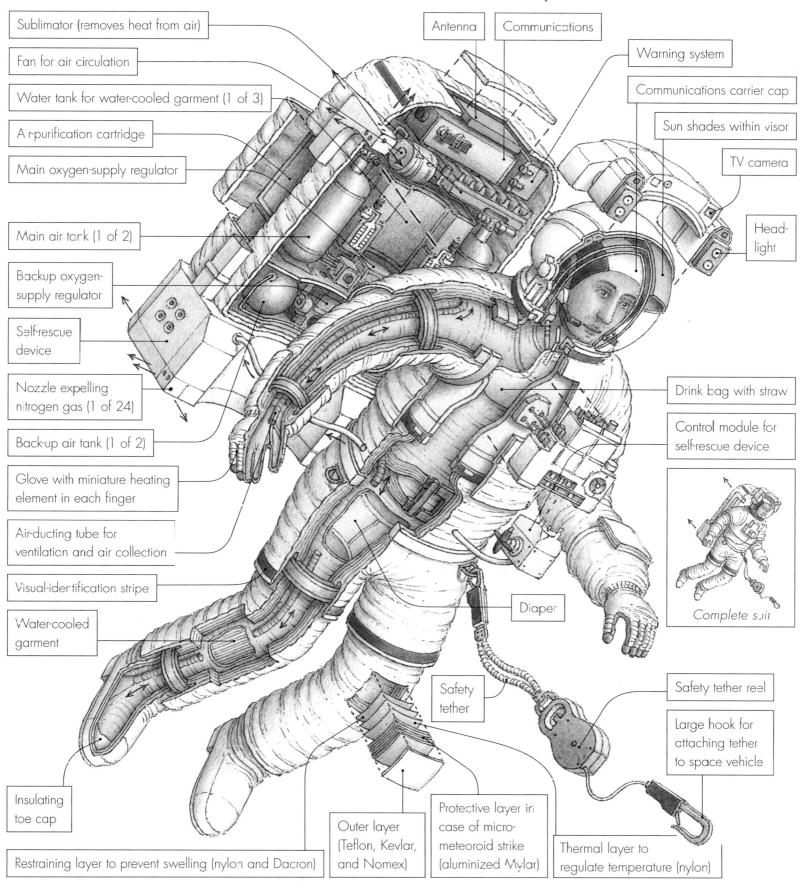

Sublimator (removes heat from air)

Fan for air circulation

Water tank for water-cooled garment (1 of 3)

Air-purification cartridge

Main oxygen-supply regulator

Main air tank (1 of 2)

Backup oxygen-supply regulator

Self-rescue device

Nozzle expelling nitrogen gas (1 of 24)

Back-up air tank (1 of 2)

Glove with miniature heating element in each finger

Air-ducting tube for ventilation and air collection

Visual-identification stripe

Water-cooled garment

Insulating toe cap

Restraining layer to prevent swelling (nylon and Dacron)

Antenna

Communications

Warning system

Communications carrier cap

Sun shades within visor

TV camera

Head-light

Drink bag with straw

Control module for self-rescue device

Complete suit

Diaper

Safety tether

Safety tether reel

Large hook for attaching tether to space vehicle

Outer layer (Teflon, Kevlar, and Nomex)

Protective layer in case of micro-meteoroid strike (aluminized Mylar)

Thermal layer to regulate temperature (nylon)

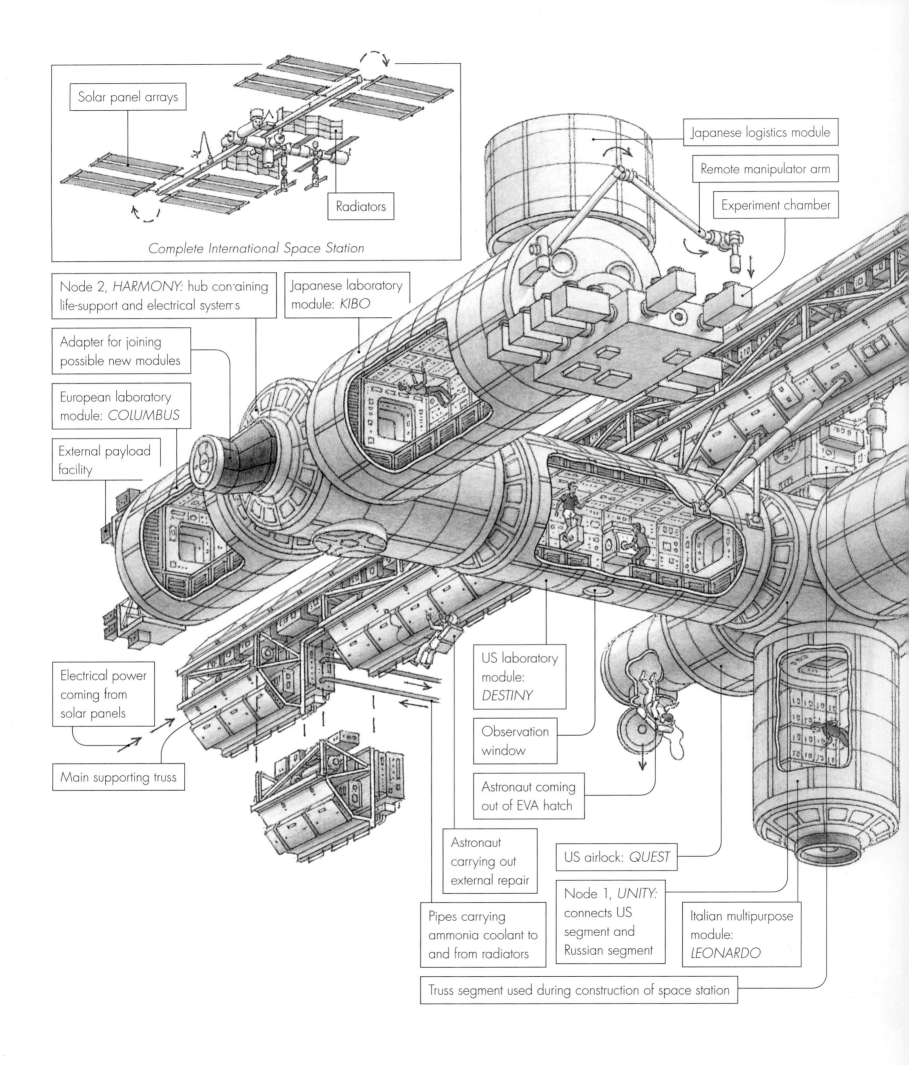

Solar panel arrays

Radiators

Complete International Space Station

Japanese logistics module

Remote manipulator arm

Experiment chamber

Node 2, *HARMONY*: hub containing life-support and electrical systems

Japanese laboratory module: *KIBO*

Adapter for joining possible new modules

European laboratory module: *COLUMBUS*

External payload facility

Electrical power coming from solar panels

Main supporting truss

US laboratory module: *DESTINY*

Observation window

Astronaut coming out of EVA hatch

Astronaut carrying out external repair

US airlock: *QUEST*

Node 1, *UNITY*: connects US segment and Russian segment

Italian multipurpose module: *LEONARDO*

Pipes carrying ammonia coolant to and from radiators

Truss segment used during construction of space station

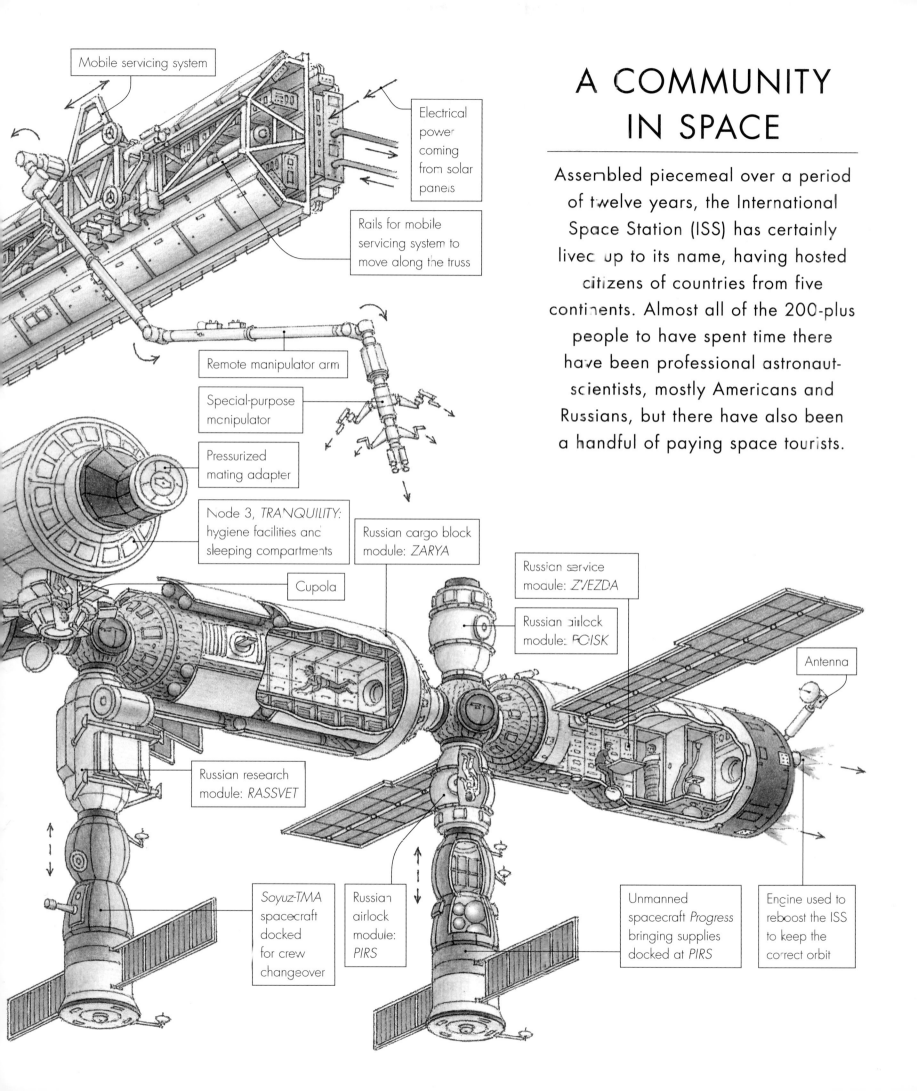

Mobile servicing system

Electrical power coming from solar panels

Rails for mobile servicing system to move along the truss

Remote manipulator arm

Special-purpose manipulator

Pressurized mating adapter

Node 3, *TRANQUILITY*: hygiene facilities and sleeping compartments

Cupola

Russian cargo block module: *ZARYA*

Russian service module: *ZVEZDA*

Russian airlock module: *POISK*

Antenna

Russian research module: *RASSVET*

Soyuz-TMA spacecraft docked for crew changeover

Russian airlock module: *PIRS*

Unmanned spacecraft *Progress* bringing supplies docked at *PIRS*

Engine used to reboost the ISS to keep the correct orbit

A COMMUNITY IN SPACE

Assembled piecemeal over a period of twelve years, the International Space Station (ISS) has certainly lived up to its name, having hosted citizens of countries from five continents. Almost all of the 200-plus people to have spent time there have been professional astronaut-scientists, mostly Americans and Russians, but there have also been a handful of paying space tourists.

The pressure of the atmosphere is as important to us as what's in it. If it's too low, or thin, we can't extract enough oxygen from it for our bodies to function. The greater the altitude, the thinner the atmosphere becomes. The atmospheric pressure at the top of the world's highest mountain, Mount Everest, is only about one-third of the pressure at sea level, 29,000 feet (9 kilometers) below. It's not surprising that it's pretty hard to breathe up there. Higher still and it becomes impossible—you need an extra supply of oxygen to stay alive. By the time you've gotten to around 30 miles (48 kilometers) up, the atmospheric pressure is only around one-thousandth that at sea level. Above that, space is very nearly a vacuum—there's hardly anything there at all.

There is some stuff, though. Inside the solar system, there are hot particles known as plasma that come from the sun and make up solar wind, and minute amounts of dust, probably mostly from comets and asteroids colliding with each

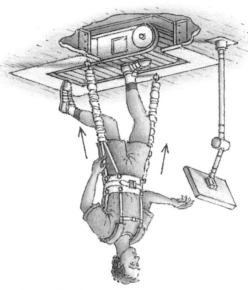

EXERCISING

other. And there are cosmic rays that pour through our solar system from other parts of the universe.

There's also light and other forms of radiation—such as radio waves and X-rays—almost all from the sun. This radiation creates heat as well as light. Without it, the earth would be a very cold place indeed. The temperature of the earth is yet another thing we tend to take for granted. In fact, we humans are very particular about the temperature of our surroundings—it can't be too hot or too cold. Ideally it should be somewhere in the seventies Fahrenheit. We can of course survive in places that are hotter or colder than that, but only if we protect ourselves. Without protection, we would die in a few minutes in temperatures of more

than 130°F (55°C) and, usually, in less than a day in temperatures of less than 50°F (10°C).

In most places on Earth, most of the time, the temperature is OK for us—neither too hot nor too cold. One very important reason for this is the distance from the sun to the earth. The amount of radiation the earth receives from the sun depends on this distance. If the sun were much closer, there would be too much radiation and it would become impossibly hot; if it were a lot farther away, there would be too little, and we would freeze.

Actually, there's more to it than that. There are other objects in space roughly the same distance from the sun as the earth is, such as the earth's moon. They receive the same amount of radiation, but their temperatures are much more extreme. Parts of the moon's surface that are

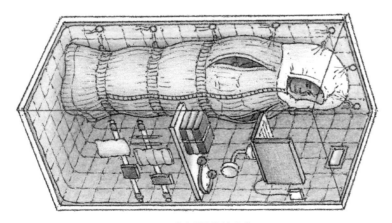

SLEEPING

EATING

USING THE TOILET

EXPERIMENTING

in full sunlight can reach over 392°F (200°C), while parts in shadow, facing away from the sun, can be colder than -328°F (-200°C).

We have mainly the atmosphere, but also the seas, the polar ice caps, and vegetation to thank for the fact that conditions aren't like this on Earth. These things all act together in a very complicated way that we still don't completely understand, bouncing some of the sun's heat back into space, soaking up and storing the rest, and spreading it out across the globe so that temperatures all over the earth stay reasonable. Even so, there are places, such as Antarctica and many deserts, where the cold or the heat make it difficult for people to survive for any length of time.

Conditions not just on the moon but in space are much more extreme than those anywhere on the earth's surface. In order to survive for even a short time away from the earth and its atmosphere, an astronaut needs protection from the heat and cold, as well as a supply of breathable air at the right pressure. For astronauts to get by for any longer, other things have to be thought about: drinking, going to the bathroom, eating, and sleeping. For longer stays, things to consider include staying fit and healthy, keeping clean, and not going insane.

The first astronauts were in space for only a short time. They stayed within a couple hundred miles of the earth's surface and remained strapped in their space capsules. But even they needed those capsules to be incredibly well insulated, and to

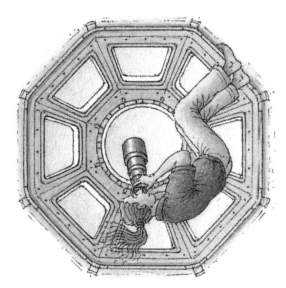

EARTH-WATCHING

have a reliable air system that supplied oxygen for them to breathe in and removed the poisonous carbon dioxide that they breathed out.

Nowadays, stays of weeks or months in orbiting space stations have become quite common. And astronauts have also gotten used to leaving the relative safety of their space vehicles and going for space walks. All this has placed more and more demands on the spacecraft and equipment used.

In fact it hasn't turned out to be too difficult, though it is incredibly expensive, to provide people with what they need for quite long periods in space. In some ways, it's like equipping a submarine or a base at the South Pole. But there's one thing that makes life in space very different from life down here. Whether orbiting in a space station or traveling to the moon, astronauts are basically weightless, as is everything around them. There's no up or down, which means it's impossible to fall, as there's nowhere to fall to. Anything that isn't firmly attached to the walls of the spaceship itself is likely to start floating around. That includes any liquids that get spilled, which hang as globules in midair.

It takes some getting used to. About half of all astronauts suffer from space sickness—very like motion sickness. Luckily it usually lasts only a few days. Soon most astronauts get the hang of floating everywhere instead of walking, but there are plenty of other things they have to get used to. Drinks can't be drunk from a cup or can, but instead must be sucked out of plastic bags with a straw. Similarly, food, which is mostly pre-prepared, is usually eaten straight out of its packet with a long-handled spoon. It's often sticky so that it will stay together and on the spoon instead of floating off before it's reached the astronaut's mouth. To sleep, the astronauts use sleeping bags tethered to the walls—they could sleep in midair, but they might bump into delicate equipment or accidentally switch off an important computer while floating around.

Washing is quite tricky. Showers are not practical, as it's hard to clear the water away afterward. Besides, water is a very precious commodity in space. Like everything else, it has to be carried there from Earth, which makes it incredibly expensive (thousands of dollars a gallon). Astronauts go through as little of it as possible, using damp cloths and wet wipes to keep clean. Going to the bathroom is also very different. Instead of a flush, which wouldn't work in any case, the toilet uses a powerful fan that acts as a vacuum hose, sucking the waste away into plastic bags.

Weightlessness makes getting around in space very easy—too easy for astronauts' bodies, which are designed to cope with gravity. Without having to bear weight, muscles and bones, especially in the back and legs, quickly start to waste away. To help make up for this, astronauts on the ISS spend over two hours a day exercising on different machines. They still tend to get skinny legs and puffy faces because fluids build up in their upper bodies. It's hard to do anything about this, but, like most other changes, it quickly goes into reverse when astronauts return to Earth.

There are, however, some longer-term risks to spending any length of time in space. Cosmic rays and solar wind can seriously damage the cells in the human body, increasing the chance of cancer and, probably, eye conditions such as cataracts. On Earth we are protected from their worst effects by the magnetosphere, an invisible field created by the earth's core acting as a kind of giant magnet.

Out in space there is no such protection. That's one of the main reasons why governments have limited the total amount of time astronauts are allowed to spend in space. So far this seems to have worked well, and most of them have continued to live healthy lives long after their space careers have finished. Whether space travelers would stay equally healthy after a really long space voyage—one to Mars, say—is a very different question.

Dehydrated spicy noodles

Vacuum-packed coated nuts

Orange drink

Canned lamb-and-vegetable stew

Vacuum-packed granola bar

Everything that astronauts eat or drink comes in its own special packaging; otherwise it would just float away.

The Huygens *space probe landed on the surface of Titan, Saturn's biggest moon, in 2005.*

IS THERE ANYBODY OUT THERE?

It's risky and very expensive getting humans to space. Once there, we need somewhere tolerable to live, away from which we have to wear big, unwieldy space suits that make it difficult for us to move and work. It's probably not very healthy for us to stay there for long periods. And there's always the problem of getting us safely back home.

Machines are different. It's relatively easy—and much cheaper—to get them there in the first place; they can stay there indefinitely and can go on working as long as their fuel supplies hold up; they can cope with heat and cold much better than we can; they don't need special breathing equipment or protection from the vacuum of space; and they don't usually have to return to Earth.

It's not surprising, then, that most of the exploration of the solar system so far has been carried out by remote-controlled space probes and robots designed to cope with the conditions away from planet Earth. These machines can make observations, take measurements, and sometimes even carry out experiments without any humans around, and then send the results back to Earth.

One of the biggest questions—for many people *the* biggest question—that these probes have been trying to help answer is: Does life in a form that we could recognize exist anywhere else in the solar system? The earliest probes carried little scientific equipment, but even they could give an idea of whether the things needed for life might be present. These, as far as we know, are liquid water, the chemical elements carbon and nitrogen, and a source of energy. For there to be liquid water, as opposed to solid ice or gassy water vapor, temperatures usually have to be similar to those on Earth. The most obvious—and easiest—places to start looking for these things were those parts of the solar system nearest to us: the moon and the two nearby planets, Venus and Mars.

By the 1950s, no one seriously expected to find life on the moon—astronomers could tell that it had no atmosphere and that any water that might once have existed on its surface would have long since evaporated. Venus and Mars were different. Of all the known planets in the solar system, they are the ones most like Earth, of roughly the same size and apparently made of pretty much the same stuff. They are also a similar distance from the sun as Earth, with Mars a bit farther away and Venus a bit closer. That means they receive similar amounts of heat from the sun as the earth, which in turn meant that it was possible that they were a similar temperature.

In the first few years of space exploration much of the attention was focused on Venus, which comes quite a lot closer to us than Mars. Efforts to study the planet directly from Earth had proven frustrating. When astronomers trained their telescopes on it, they could not make out any features, such as mountains or craters, as they could with our moon or Mars or even Mercury. The simplest explanation was that the planet was covered in a thick layer of clouds. Because it is closer to the sun than us, people imagined that it might be a steamy, jungly place, like a hotter version of the earth's tropics, perhaps even populated by Venusians. By the late 1950s, advances in astronomy had begun to cast doubt on this notion. New telescopes that used microwaves seemed to show that the planet's surface was far too hot for liquid water to be present, making it very unlikely to be inhabited. But it was hard to be absolutely certain. Perhaps a space probe equipped with temperature sensors might answer the question once and for all.

Venus is close to Earth compared with the other planets, but it's not that close. At its nearest it's about 24 million miles (39 million kilometers) away, more than a hundred times farther than the moon. Small wonder, then, that the first attempts to get a working spaceship there, undertaken by the Soviet Union in 1961, failed. Success wasn't long in coming, though. The US spacecraft *Mariner 2*, launched in August 1962, got to within 22,000 miles (35,000 kilometers) of the planet in December, before hurtling past to go into orbit around the sun. Information from its sensors confirmed that Venus's surface was indeed too hot for life, with a temperature that we now know is over 750°F (400°C).

Further journeys to Venus have all confirmed what an extreme place the planet is. Not only is its surface incredibly hot, but its atmosphere—a poisonous mixture of carbon dioxide with added sulfuric acid—is very dense, with a pressure at the surface nearly one hundred times that on Earth (it's this thick atmosphere that traps the sun's heat, which is why the planet is so hot). The first probes sent to land on the surface were launched before anyone realized this, and were all crushed before they reached the ground. Later probes were stronger, and several have successfully landed, though none has survived more than a couple of hours in the horrendous conditions. Recent unmanned crafts, like the European Space Agency's *Venus Express,* have orbited the planet from a safe distance, gathering much intriguing information about its atmosphere, which turns out to be wild and stormy, with frequent lightning and 250-mph (400-kph) winds.

As with Venus, the earliest attempts to get a spacecraft anywhere near Mars failed. The first successful probe was the American *Mariner 4*, which came to within 6,000 miles (9,700 kilometers) of the planet's surface in July 1965, following a seven-month journey from Earth. Any

Over one billion kilometers from Earth, the space probe Cassini *passes by the southern pole of Enceladus, one of Saturn's most mysterious moons and one of the places in the solar system where alien life might conceivably exist.*

hopes that it would find obvious signs of life were quickly dashed. *Mariner 4*'s sensors showed the planet's surface to be a dry, cold, barren place, with a thin carbon dioxide atmosphere a hundred times less dense than Earth's.

Even though daytime temperatures can sometimes reach 70°F (20°C) or more, that lack of a breathable atmosphere makes Mars a pretty inhospitable place. Still, it's been much easier to build machines that can deal with the conditions there than ones that can operate on Venus. As a result, Mars has become the main destination for interplanetary exploration. So far, more than fifty Mars-bound missions have taken place, with more planned. There have been numerous failures, but also spectacular successes, including the landing by NASA of four rovers, most recently *Curiosity* in 2012.

These and other probes have continued to make fascinating discoveries. They've found evidence that Mars was once wetter and warmer than it is today. They've also shown that a large amount of water is still present underground, with clear signs that it sometimes comes to the surface, lasting long enough there to flow down slopes and along gulleys. Exactly how this happens has been a puzzle — water should either freeze solid or quickly evaporate in the thin Martian atmosphere.

Scientists now believe they've found the answer. It's thought that on Mars the water combines with chemicals called perchlorates to form salty solutions that stay liquid at much lower temperatures than pure water does. These solutions are probably present underground all the time, seeping to the surface at night when it's cold and then evaporating as it warms up during the day. The solutions themselves are believed to be too cold to support the kind of life found on Earth. It's possible that water exists in a different, warmer form deep underground, but we don't know that at the moment. All this means that we can't say for certain there is no life on Mars, but if it's there, it's almost certainly deep underground, and is going to be pretty hard to find.

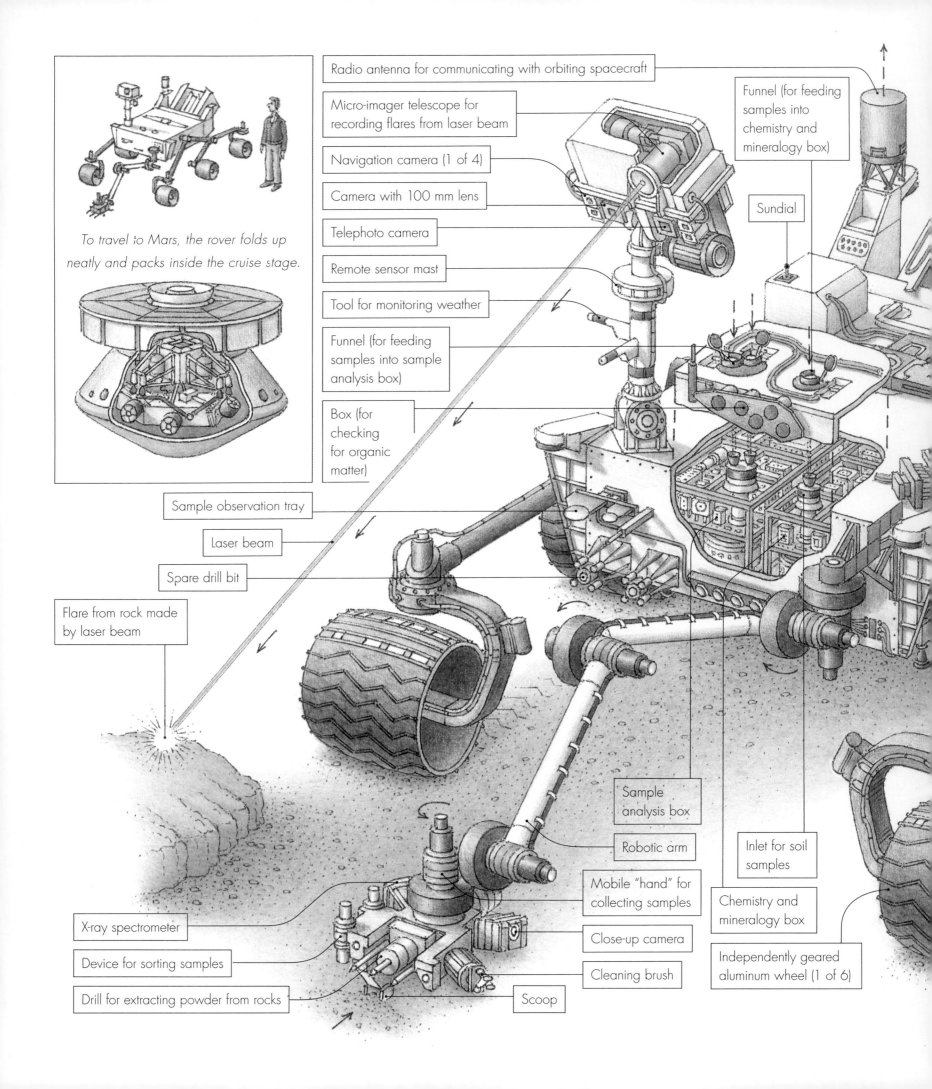

To travel to Mars, the rover folds up neatly and packs inside the cruise stage.

Radio antenna for communicating with orbiting spacecraft

Micro-imager telescope for recording flares from laser beam

Navigation camera (1 of 4)

Camera with 100 mm lens

Telephoto camera

Remote sensor mast

Tool for monitoring weather

Funnel (for feeding samples into sample analysis box)

Box (for checking for organic matter)

Sample observation tray

Laser beam

Spare drill bit

Flare from rock made by laser beam

X-ray spectrometer

Device for sorting samples

Drill for extracting powder from rocks

Funnel (for feeding samples into chemistry and mineralogy box)

Sundial

Sample analysis box

Robotic arm

Mobile "hand" for collecting samples

Close-up camera

Cleaning brush

Scoop

Inlet for soil samples

Chemistry and mineralogy box

Independently geared aluminum wheel (1 of 6)

A ROBOT ON MARS

It might look like a glorified dune buggy, but the Mars *Curiosity* rover is one of the most sophisticated pieces of machinery ever. It's a mobile laboratory, weather station, camera, and communications center, capable of analyzing samples of Martian rock and soil and sending the results millions of miles back to Earth. Its discoveries have revolutionized our understanding of our chilly, barren neighbor.

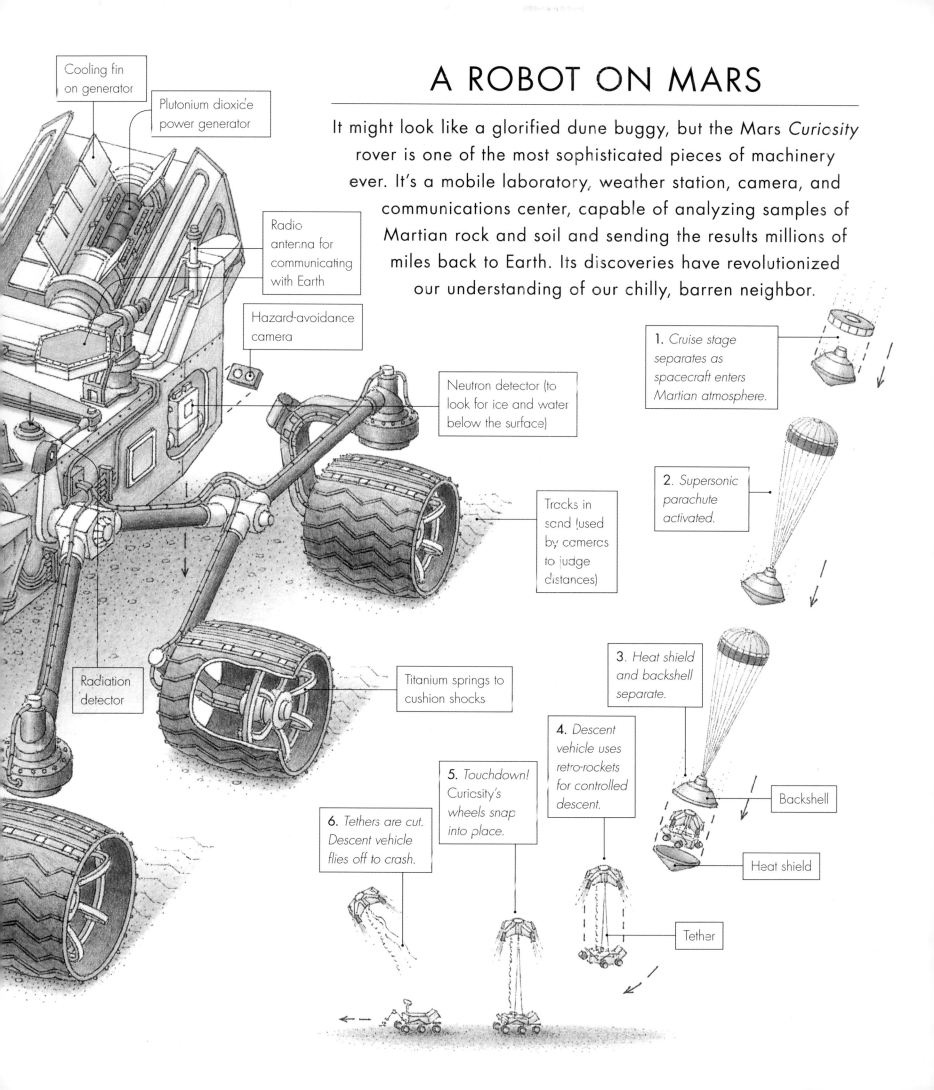

Cooling fin on generator

Plutonium dioxide power generator

Radio antenna for communicating with Earth

Hazard-avoidance camera

Neutron detector (to look for ice and water below the surface)

Tracks in sand (used by cameras to judge distances)

Radiation detector

Titanium springs to cushion shocks

1. *Cruise stage separates as spacecraft enters Martian atmosphere.*

2. *Supersonic parachute activated.*

3. *Heat shield and backshell separate.*

4. *Descent vehicle uses retro-rockets for controlled descent.*

5. *Touchdown! Curiosity's wheels snap into place.*

6. *Tethers are cut. Descent vehicle flies off to crash.*

Backshell

Heat shield

Tether

And what about elsewhere in the solar system? Mercury, the tiny planet nearest the sun, like our moon, has no atmosphere and has a surface that seems to be either incredibly hot or incredibly cold, with virtually nothing in between. The giant planets far out in the solar system, Jupiter, Saturn, Uranus, and Neptune, do have atmospheres, but they're mainly made of hydrogen and helium. We don't know exactly what conditions are like deeper down, but we do know that they must be utterly unlike Earth.

These planets are certainly not promising places to go looking for life, but some of their many moons are a different proposition. Even though a number of these moons are visible through telescopes from Earth, they were little known until space probes started venturing that far, first *Pioneer 10* and *Pioneer 11* in the early 1970s, then the *Voyagers,* and more recently *Cassini-Huygens,* launched in 1997. The discoveries they've made have created huge interest and excitement back here on Earth.

One of the best-studied moons is Saturn's Titan, the second-biggest moon in the solar system, bigger than the planet Mercury. Amazingly, the probe *Huygens* actually landed on its surface in 2005, sending back photos and other information for 90 minutes before its power ran out. That's amazing because Titan is 900 million miles (1.5 billion kilometers) from Earth.

The pictures *Huygens* sent back showed what an alien place Titan is. On its surface, it's extremely cold—around -300°F (-185°C). It's the only moon in the solar system with a thick atmosphere, mainly made up of nitrogen (like Earth's), and it's the only known place in the solar system other than Earth to have large amounts of liquid on its surface. In this case, though, the liquid isn't water but hydrocarbons—chemical compounds of hydrogen and carbon—especially methane and ethane. There is water on Titan too, but, on the surface at least, it's frozen into rock-like ice. There are theories, though, that deep underground there may be a supercooled sludgy ocean of water mixed with the chemical ammonia, similar to the perchlorate-water solutions we think exist on Mars.

Titan seems to be far too cold for any Earth-like life to exist there. However, some scientists have suggested that there could be life-forms present that use liquid methane instead of water. It's a radical idea, but it's not impossible.

Not much heat from the sun gets this far out into the solar system, and all the other moons of Saturn and Jupiter, not to mention the even more distant Uranus and Neptune, have deadly cold surfaces, just as Titan does. Space probes have indicated that most of them are giant lumps of rock or ice frozen through and through. But some evidently aren't. Of these, perhaps the most intriguing is Enceladus, which, like Titan, is one of Saturn's moons.

Enceladus is tiny—just 310 miles (500 kilometers) across. It had attracted little attention until *Cassini-Huygens* arrived there in 2004. While *Huygens* detached to make its one-way trip to Titan, *Cassini* went into orbit around Saturn. It's been orbiting there ever since and has gathered lots of information about the planet's rings, its stormy atmosphere, and its moons. It has passed by Enceladus many times. Among the first things it photographed there were enormous trails of vapor coming from the moon's southern pole. It turns out that these are produced by geysers spewing water at the rate of 550 pounds (250 kilograms) a second. *Cassini*'s sensors have shown that this part of the moon is much warmer than its north pole and almost certainly has a salty ocean of liquid water under the ice where the water vapor comes from. The sensors have also found carbon-based chemicals in the vapor. No one yet has a good explanation for why this part of the moon is so warm—by rights it should have frozen solid long ago.

Enceladus is not the only moon that may have a watery ocean beneath its surface—Jupiter's moons Ganymede (the largest moon in the solar system), Europa, and Callisto are three others. But Enceladus is the one for which the evidence at the moment is the strongest, and the place that scientists think is the most likely, of all the ones we've looked at so far, to harbor some form of alien life.

SPACE EXPLORERS

A whole range of different space probes has been used to explore the solar system, each one carefully designed for its particular mission.

PIONEER 10 *was the first probe to visit Jupiter, flying past in 1973 after a 21-month journey and taking remarkable close-up photos of the solar system's biggest planet.*

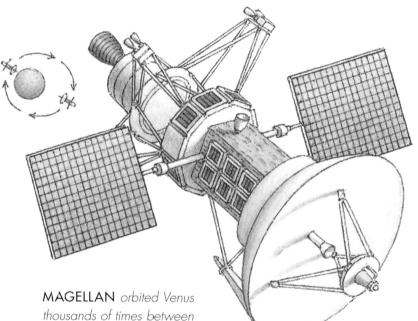

MAGELLAN *orbited Venus thousands of times between 1990 and 1994, producing what is still the best map of the planet's surface.*

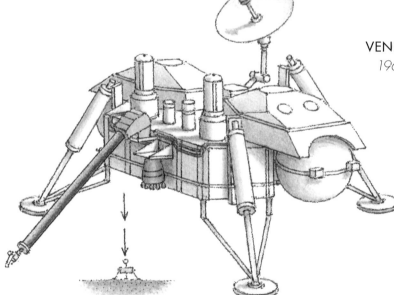

VENERA 4 *successfully penetrated Venus's hot, dense atmosphere in October 1967, transmitting valuable data for 93 minutes before ceasing to function.*

VIKING 1 *was one of two identical Viking probes to make a soft landing on Mars in 1976; it worked until the end of 1982.*

LUNOKHOD 1 *was a rover that landed on Earth's moon in 1970 and was intended to pave the way for manned Soviet moon missions, which in the end never took place.*

ARTIFICIAL MOONS

The earth has only one natural satellite — the moon — but now has thousands of artificial ones, in different orbits and doing a range of different jobs. Most satellites have nearly circular orbits, but some have highly eccentric ones, swooping close to the earth and then far out again, like comets orbiting the sun.

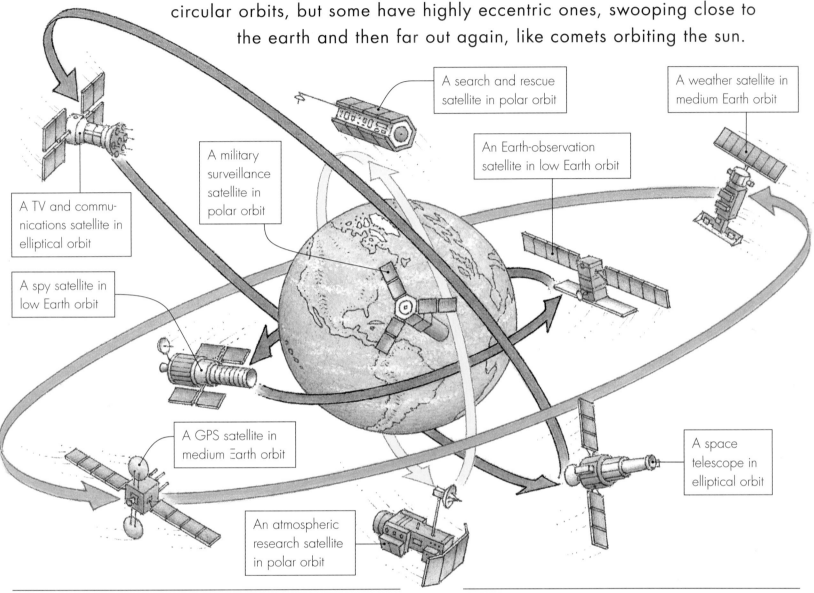

A search and rescue satellite in polar orbit

A weather satellite in medium Earth orbit

A military surveillance satellite in polar orbit

An Earth-observation satellite in low Earth orbit

A TV and communications satellite in elliptical orbit

A spy satellite in low Earth orbit

A space telescope in elliptical orbit

A GPS satellite in medium Earth orbit

An atmospheric research satellite in polar orbit

STAYING ON COURSE

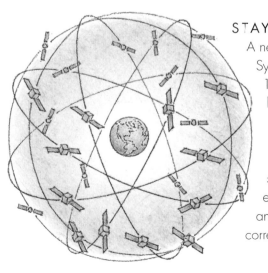

A network of Global Positioning System (GPS) satellites orbiting 12,500 miles (20,000 kilometers) up continuously feeds information to a car's driver using a satellite navigation system. A control station on the ground keeps exact track of each satellite and sends small course corrections directly to the driver.

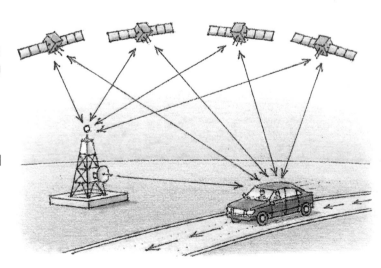

an awful lot of people driving around hopelessly lost. They're hugely important in communications too, being used for many phone, TV, and Internet links. They provide vital information on the state of our planet, keeping track of all sorts of things—from the daily weather to how much ice there is in the Arctic to how big the hole in the ozone layer is. And they're used more and more to keep tabs on what people everywhere are doing.

Where they are up there exactly depends on which job they are doing. Some, like the International Space Station (ISS) and almost all of the space telescopes, are in low Earth orbit, circling the earth a couple hundred miles up. The ones used in navigation, called Global Positioning System (GPS) satellites, are in medium Earth orbit, around 12,500 miles (20,000 kilometers) from the earth's surface. And then there are a whole lot more farther away still—in high Earth orbit—at 22,236 miles (35,786 kilometers) above sea level, to be precise; this is where most of the ones used in communications are found.

Why 22,236 miles exactly? Well, it's all about physics. Because of gravity, an object orbiting around the earth a particular distance away will stay circling at that distance provided that it's going at the right speed and unless something stops it. When it's doing this, it's in what is called a stable orbit. The right speed for a stable orbit depends on how far away from the center of the earth the object is—the farther away, the slower the speed.

The ISS is in orbit at just over 250 miles (400 kilometers) above sea level, which is just over 4,200 miles (6,760 kilometers) from the center of the earth. The speed of a stable orbit at this distance is 17,150 mph (27,600 kph). Traveling that fast that far away from the earth, the station makes a complete orbit once every 93 minutes. The earth itself takes just under 24 hours to spin on its own axis. This is what's called a sidereal day. By the time the earth has done this, the station has been around the earth fifteen and a half times. At 22,236 miles above sea level, where the high Earth orbit satellites are, the speed of stable orbit is about 6,900 mph (11,000 kph).

At that speed, the satellites make one complete orbit of the earth in exactly one sidereal day.

Orbits of this kind are called geosynchronous. A satellite in geosynchronous orbit is always at exactly the same spot in the sky at the same time every single day. If, on the other hand, the satellite is orbiting along the line of the earth's equator, then it stays directly above the same spot on the ground the entire time. It is in what is known as a geostationary orbit. Viewed through a telescope, a satellite in geostationary orbit doesn't seem to move at all, unlike everything else in the sky.

Geostationary orbits are incredibly useful because the antennas on the ground used to pick up their signals don't have to move—they can be pointed at the spot in the sky where the satellite is. So, while the satellites themselves are expensive and quite tricky to launch, and you need a powerful signal to keep in touch with them that far away, the system as a whole is reliable and relatively cheap to run.

And what about the Global Positioning System satellites, the ones that are used in navigation? They make a circuit of the earth in exactly 12 hours—they're in semi-synchronous orbit, returning to the same spot overhead twice every day. A GPS system has a very accurate clock, and it knows exactly where these satellites should be in their orbits at any moment. It receives signals from them and can use this information to figure out exactly where it is, and it can show its location on a map stored in its system. Using its computer, it can also figure out the best route to a particular destination and, by continuously updating itself, guide its user there.

All this might seem very modern and high-tech, but the principle isn't that different from the way sailors have navigated for centuries, except instead of satellites, they used stars, billions and billions of miles away. By recording where different stars were in the night sky and knowing what time it was, they could figure out where on Earth they were. Of course, they didn't have a computer to tell them what route to follow. They had to decide that for themselves.

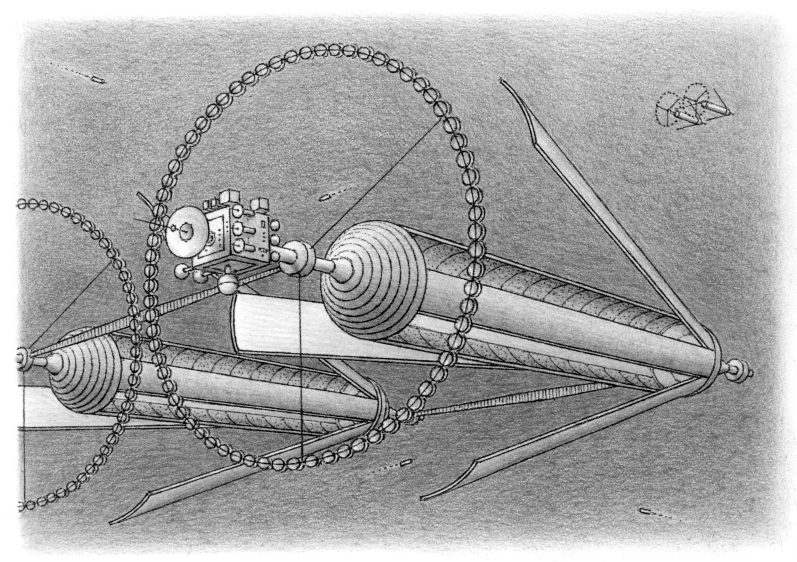

An O'Neill cylinder — an imagined, 20-mile- (32-kilometer-) long home for people in space

WHERE DO WE GO FROM HERE?

When Neil Armstrong took his historic first step on the moon in July 1969, many people assumed that this was just the start of a great space adventure. Trips to the moon would become common, there might even be settlements there, and very soon people would be heading much farther afield, spreading out across the solar system.

It hasn't turned out that way at all. Since 1972, when the last of the Apollo missions took place, no humans have been farther into space than low Earth orbit. This is mostly because it is so expensive.

The race to put a person on the moon was just that—a race between two superpowers, the US and the Soviet Union, competing fiercely to win glory in the eyes of the world. It was also incredibly expensive. Once the race was over, both sides quickly lost interest in spending huge amounts of money in this way. The fact that Venus and Mars, our nearest planetary neighbors, turned out to be pretty inhospitable places for humans has also discouraged governments from putting a lot of effort into getting people to either of them. Attention has been devoted to other things—developing satellite technology, ground-based astronomy, and remote-controlled unmanned spacecraft. These are in some ways less glamorous, but they have delivered impressive results far more cheaply.

Life in space hasn't been abandoned completely. Over the years, several hundred astronauts have spent time on various orbiting space stations, most recently the International Space Station and China's *Tiangong 1*. And of course space exploration has lived on in people's imaginations, in films, books, TV shows, and video games.

And now there's serious talk again about getting humans back into deep space, of establishing bases on the moon and sending people to Mars. How realistic any of this is—especially getting to Mars—is a big question.

In theory, it should already be possible for humans to travel to Mars. After all, we can get robots there, we can build spacecraft that can carry people to the moon, and we know that astronauts can survive in space for the seven months that the journey would take. If we put all this together, surely a manned trip to Mars shouldn't be too difficult? That's the theory. In practice, it would be more complicated.

For a start, the humans who have spent long periods in space have all only been in low Earth orbit. A lengthy journey through deep space would be very different. In particular, astronauts on a trip to Mars would be in danger of being exposed to a lot of harmful radiation from cosmic rays and solar wind. Although it may be possible to shield living quarters on a spaceship using water, plastic, or liquid hydrogen (which would double as part of the rocket fuel), no one has yet come up with a practical design.

What if we did successfully get people to Mars? Then comes the really big problem: getting them home again. To get back from Mars, astronauts would have to travel there in a vehicle that could be reused for the return journey, or bring the return vehicle with them, or build it there. Any of these would make the outbound journey much more complicated to organize.

And then there's the question of the fuel. As we know, to get back into space from the surface of a planet (or a moon), a vehicle needs energy to overcome gravity and resistance from the atmosphere. This requires fuel. The amount depends on the size of the vehicle, the thickness of the atmosphere, and how strong the gravity is, which in turn depends on the size and mass of the planet or moon.

Overcoming the earth's gravity and resistance from its atmosphere requires a huge amount of energy—that's why we need very large rockets with a lot of fuel to launch even quite small space vehicles. The moon is smaller than the earth and has much weaker gravity and no atmosphere. Launching something off its surface doesn't require that much energy—little enough that even a small vehicle like a lunar-landing module can carry the necessary fuel quite easily. Mars is between the two. It is quite a lot smaller than the earth and has less than half the earth's gravity at its surface. It also has a much thinner atmosphere, which means less air resistance. But it would still take an awful lot more energy to launch a vehicle from Mars's surface than it would from the moon.

The fuel for this would either have to be carried from Earth or gotten from Mars. Carrying it from Earth would massively increase the weight of the outbound space vehicle and make the landing on Mars very dangerous, and we don't yet have the technology to extract or make fuel on Mars. In any case, the equipment needed would itself have to be carried from Earth.

None of this is practical at the moment. That's why people have suggested that the first manned trips to Mars are more likely to be flybys, with astronauts orbiting the planet before returning home or else landing on one of Mars's two tiny moons, which would be easy to take off from. There is another option: a one-way trip. This has been seriously proposed, and quite a few people have even put their names down for just such an adventure, though who knows how many would really be prepared to go when the time came.

A HOME ON MARS?

It's a long way off, but if we humans ever did settle on Mars, a colony might look something like this. Unlike Earth, Mars has no magnetosphere to protect its inhabitants from harmful cosmic rays and solar radiation, so any settlement would have to be well shielded. Just as on our moon or in space, anyone venturing outside would have to wear a protective suit with a breathing apparatus.

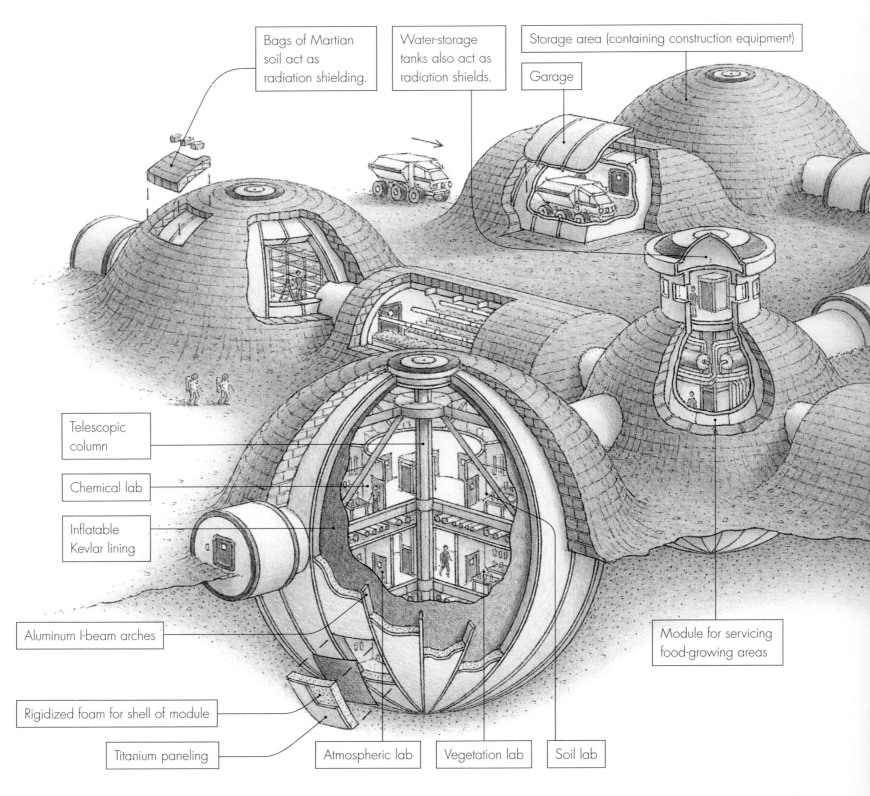

Bags of Martian soil act as radiation shielding.

Water-storage tanks also act as radiation shields.

Storage area (containing construction equipment)

Garage

Telescopic column

Chemical lab

Inflatable Kevlar lining

Aluminum I-beam arches

Module for servicing food-growing areas

Rigidized foam for shell of module

Titanium paneling

Atmospheric lab

Vegetation lab

Soil lab

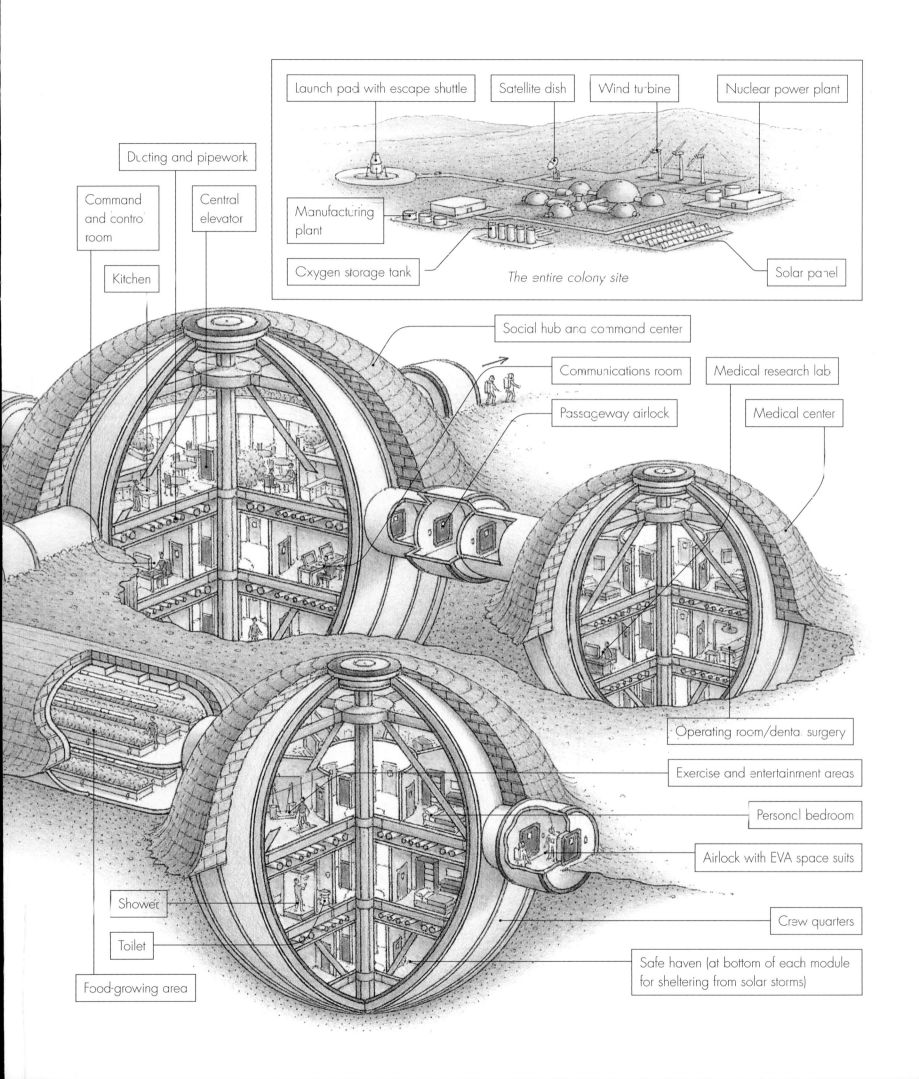

Launch pad with escape shuttle

Satellite dish

Wind turbine

Nuclear power plant

Ducting and pipework

Command and control room

Central elevator

Manufacturing plant

Kitchen

Oxygen storage tank

The entire colony site

Solar panel

Social hub and command center

Communications room

Medical research lab

Medical center

Passageway airlock

Operating room/dental surgery

Exercise and entertainment areas

Personal bedroom

Airlock with EVA space suits

Shower

Crew quarters

Toilet

Safe haven (at bottom of each module for sheltering from solar storms)

Food-growing area

Realistically, any of these ventures is still only a pretty distant possibility. Quite a lot of people think it would be more sensible to try to establish a base on the moon first, perhaps underground. Since it's so much easier to take off and land from there than it is from Earth, this would serve as a very useful jumping-off point for farther journeys. Of course, it would still mean that everything would have to be transported there from the earth in the first place. And currently that requires using expensive and wasteful rockets.

The prospects for extended space travel might change dramatically if a better way of getting stuff into space in the first place could be found. One of the most exciting ideas proposed is a space elevator—a cable stretching thousands of miles into space to a platform in geostationary orbit that could be used for raising and lowering

loads. It sounds utterly far-fetched but, in theory at least, it's possible. It would be extremely expensive to build, but once up and running, it would be a far cheaper way than rockets of getting people, machinery, and fuel into space.

With a space elevator, it might become possible to build spacecraft that could carry people out to the far planets and moons of the solar system. Inventors have even proposed space colonies—artificial worlds moving through space that by spinning, could create gravity and could house thousands of people.

None of these things is going to happen very soon, and they may not ever happen at all. It may prove simply too expensive and technically too difficult to build a space elevator, for example. But it's not absolutely impossible that, in a few hundred years, say, humans could be spread throughout the solar system.

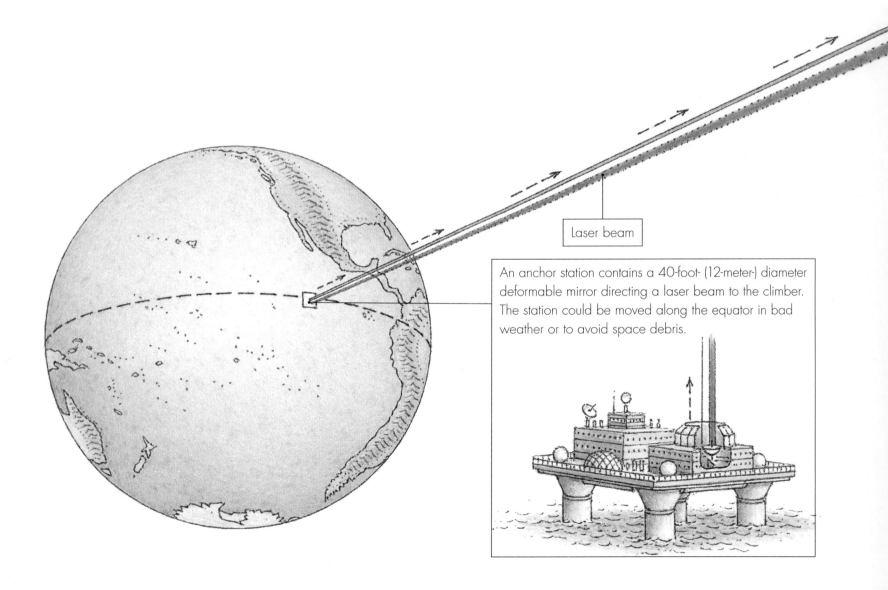

Laser beam

An anchor station contains a 40-foot- (12-meter-) diameter deformable mirror directing a laser beam to the climber. The station could be moved along the equator in bad weather or to avoid space debris.

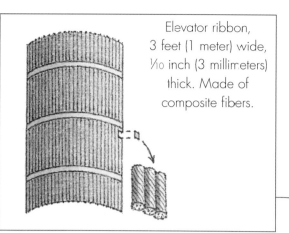

Elevator ribbon, 3 feet (1 meter) wide, 1/10 inch (3 millimeters) thick. Made of composite fibers.

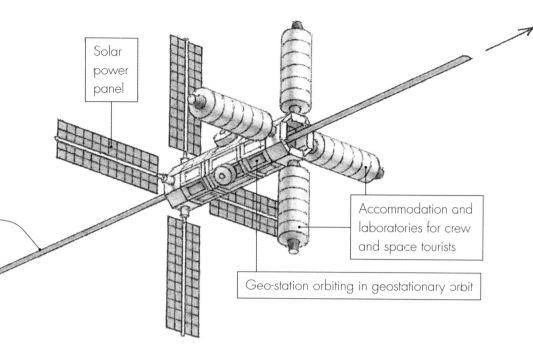

Solar power panel

Accommodation and laboratories for crew and space tourists

Geo-station orbiting in geostationary orbit

Photovoltaic cells convert the laser beam into electricity to power the climber.

A climber, with a 30-person crew and a passenger module on top of a cargo module, ascends the cable at 125 mph (200 kph), taking 5 days to reach the geo-station. The passenger module has radiation protection for passing through the Van Allen belts.

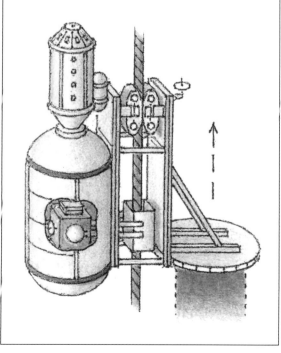

A LIFT INTO SPACE?

If we ever get as far as settling on Mars, the chances are we will have built something like a space elevator first. Much of the technology already exists, but it would be an incredibly ambitious and expensive undertaking, and no one really knows whether one could ever be made to work in practice.

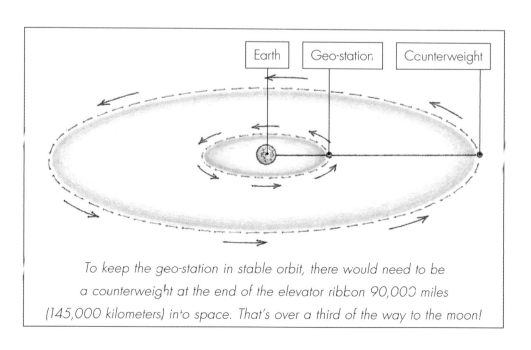

Earth   Geo-station   Counterweight

To keep the geo-station in stable orbit, there would need to be a counterweight at the end of the elevator ribbon 90,000 miles (145,000 kilometers) into space. That's over a third of the way to the moon!

And what about farther afield? What are the chances of us humans ever visiting any of the other billions and billions of stars and their attendant planets that we know are out there? Now we really are dreaming. The distances are simply too huge, and the laws of physics are against us. Remember that *Voyager 1* will take 30,000 years to reach the outer edge of the solar system, which is less than half the distance from here to the next nearest star system. We might be able to build spaceships that could go quite a lot faster than *Voyager 1*, but there is no known technology that could significantly reduce the journey time. Because unless we've got our understanding of physics completely wrong, there's an absolute limit on how fast anything can travel in the universe, and that's at the speed of light. Even traveling at nearly

that speed, a spaceship would be able to explore only the tiniest corner of one tiny corner of one arm of the Milky Way galaxy in many human lifetimes.

We shouldn't be downhearted, though. We can travel as far as we like in our imaginations. And we can do something else. Just as we have already built telescopes that span continents using interferometry, we could in theory build ones that spread across the whole solar system. Such telescopes would allow us to view other parts of the universe in incredible detail. Who knows what, or who, we might discover out there? And of course the more we find out about other worlds, the more we might come to appreciate how unique and precious our planet that we call home really is.

INDEX

TIME LINE: Discovering Space

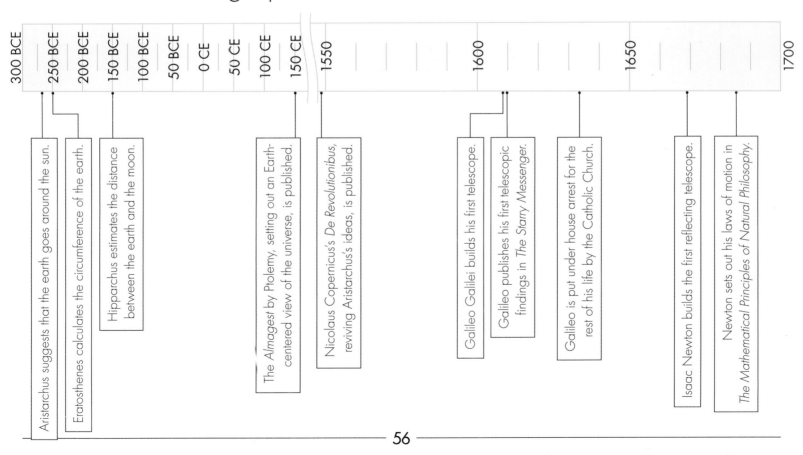

300 BCE — 250 BCE — 200 BCE — 150 BCE — 100 BCE — 50 BCE — 0 CE — 50 CE — 100 CE — 150 CE — 1550 — 1600 — 1650 — 1700

Aristarchus suggests that the earth goes around the sun.

Eratosthenes calculates the circumference of the earth.

Hipparchus estimates the distance between the earth and the moon.

The *Almagest* by Ptolemy, setting out an Earth-centered view of the universe, is published.

Nicolaus Copernicus's *De Revolutionibus*, reviving Aristarchus's ideas, is published.

Galileo Galilei builds his first telescope.

Galileo publishes his first telescopic findings in *The Starry Messenger*.

Galileo is put under house arrest for the rest of his life by the Catholic Church.

Isaac Newton builds the first reflecting telescope.

Newton sets out his laws of motion in *The Mathematical Principles of Natural Philosophy*.

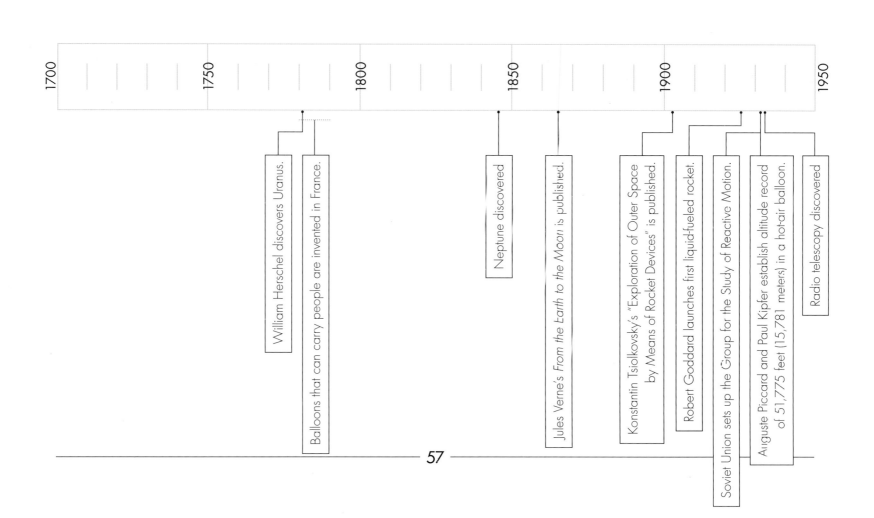

GLOSSARY

ASTEROID: a solid object considerably smaller than a planet that orbits the sun

ASTRONAUT: a person who travels into space

ASTRONOMICAL UNIT: the distance from the earth to the sun: about 93 million miles (150 million kilometers)

ASTRONOMY: the study of space and the objects in it

ATMOSPHERE: a layer of gases around an object in space such as a star, planet, or moon

COMET: an icy object similar to an asteroid that orbits the sun in an elliptical path and that glows or produces a long tail when it gets near the sun

COSMIC RAY: a stream of minute particles that travel incredibly fast through space, some of which enter the earth's atmosphere

COSMONAUT: a Russian term for an astronaut

DAY, OR SIDEREAL DAY: the time it takes for a planet to rotate once on its centerline or axis; Earth's day is just under 24 hours; Venus's day is just over 5,800 hours, or 243 Earth days

TIME LINE:

Exploring Space

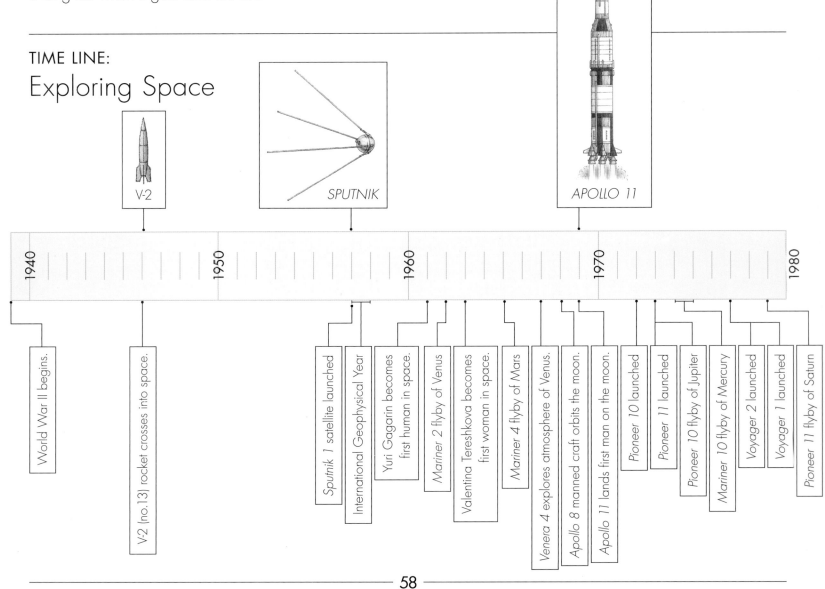

V-2

SPUTNIK

APOLLO 11

1940   1950   1960   1970   1980

World War II begins.

V-2 (no.13) rocket crosses into space.

Sputnik 1 satellite launched

International Geophysical Year

Yuri Gagarin becomes first human in space.

Mariner 2 flyby of Venus

Valentina Tereshkova becomes first woman in space.

Mariner 4 flyby of Mars

Venera 4 explores atmosphere of Venus.

Apollo 8 manned craft orbits the moon.

Apollo 11 lands first man on the moon.

Pioneer 10 launched

Pioneer 11 launched

Pioneer 10 flyby of Jupiter

Mariner 10 flyby of Mercury

Voyager 2 launched

Voyager 1 launched

Pioneer 11 flyby of Saturn

DWARF PLANET: an object that orbits the sun and is nearly as big as a planet but not quite

ELLIPSE: a flattened circle (see orbit)

GALAXY: a collection of stars and other stuff — such as interstellar gas and the remains of old stars — all traveling together through space

GRAVITY: the way in which things in the universe are attracted to one another; gravitational attraction between the sun and the planets keeps the planets in orbit around the sun, and gravitational attraction between us and the earth keeps us on the surface of the earth

HEAT SHIELD: a covering on a spacecraft that keeps the craft from getting too hot when it comes back into the earth's atmosphere

INTERSTELLAR SPACE: the universe beyond the solar system

LIGHT YEAR: the distance that light travels in one Earth year: about 5.9 trillion miles (9.5 trillion kilometers)

METEOR: a solid object from space that enters the earth's atmosphere and usually burns up entirely, also known as a shooting star

METEORITE: a lump of metal or rock that is part of the remains of a meteor that did not entirely burn up in the earth's atmosphere but fell to Earth instead

MILKY WAY: our galaxy

MOON: a solid object that orbits a planet

ORBIT: the elliptical path in space that an object makes going around a larger object; the earth orbits the sun, and the earth's moon orbits the earth

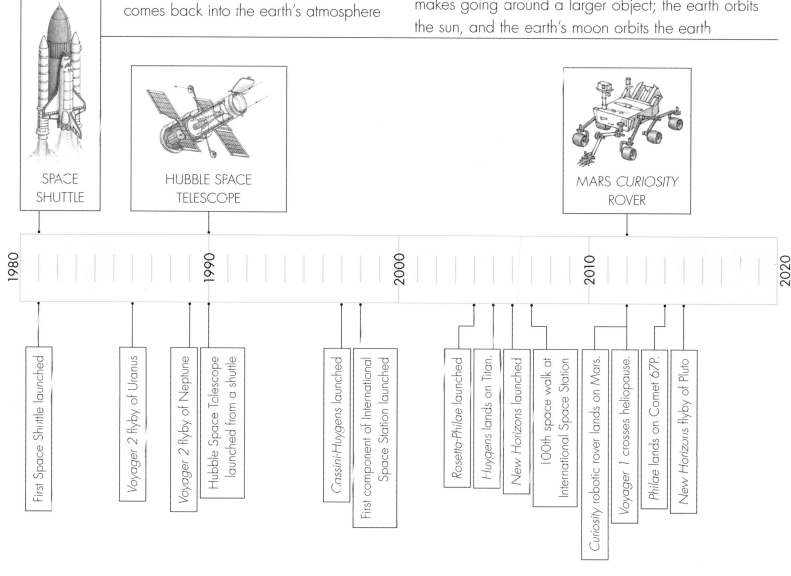

SPACE SHUTTLE

HUBBLE SPACE TELESCOPE

MARS CURIOSITY ROVER

1980

1990

2000

2010

2020

First Space Shuttle launched

Voyager 2 flyby of Uranus

Voyager 2 flyby of Neptune

Hubble Space Telescope launched from a shuttle

Cassini-Huygens launched

First component of International Space Station launched

Rosetta-Philae launched

Huygens lands on Titan.

New Horizons launched

100th space walk at International Space Station

Curiosity robotic rover lands on Mars.

Voyager 1 crosses heliopause.

Philae lands on Comet 67P.

New Horizons flyby of Pluto

PAYLOAD: the cargo that a rocket carries into space, such as a satellite, or food supplies for the International Space Station

PLANET: a large spherical object that orbits a star

PLASMA: a form of matter that is something like a gas and is almost always very hot

REENTRY: the point at which a spacecraft comes back into the earth's atmosphere

ROCKET: a vehicle or device that moves by using a rocket engine

ROCKET ENGINE: an engine that carries all its own fuel and that works by pushing out gas made by the fuel through one or more nozzles

SATELLITE: any object in space that orbits another, bigger object; the earth is a satellite of the sun, and the moon is a satellite of the earth

SOLAR SYSTEM: the part of space with the sun at the center and that is affected by the sun's gravity

SOLAR WIND: minute particles thrown out by the sun that travel very fast outward through the solar system

SPACE: the whole universe beyond the earth's atmosphere

SPACE PROBE: a machine that is sent into space to try to explore and collect data

STAR: a ball of glowing plasma in space

SUN: the star at the center of our solar system

TELESCOPE: an instrument for viewing faraway objects

UNIVERSE: all existing matter and space

YEAR: the time it takes a planet to make one complete orbit of the sun; an Earth year is 365 Earth days; a Martian year is 687 Earth days

SELECTED SOURCES

Baker, David. *International Space Station: 1998–2011*. Somerset, UK: Haynes Publishing, 2012.

———. *NASA Mars Rovers: 1997–2013 (Sojourner, Spirit, Opportunity and Curiosity)*. Somerset, UK: Haynes Publishing, 2013.

Bell, Jim. *The Space Book*. New York: Sterling Publishing, 2013.

Godwin, Robert. *Russian Spacecraft*. Burlington, ON: Collector's Guide Publishing, 2006.

———. *Hubble: Space Telescope*. Burlington, ON: Collector's Guide Publishing, 2006.

Joels, Kerry Mark, Gregory P. Kennedy, and David Larkin. *The Space Shuttle Operator's Manual*. New York: Ballantine, 1988.

Kitmacher, Gary H. *Reference Guide to the International Space Station*. N.P., n.p., 2010.

Riley, Christopher, and Phil Dolling. *NASA Apollo 11: 1969*. Somerset, UK: Haynes Publishing, 2010.

Sagan, Carl. *Cosmos*. New York: Ballantine, 2013.

Sparrow, Giles. *Spaceflight: The Complete Story from Sputnik to Shuttle — and Beyond*. New York: Dorling Kindersley, 2007.

The European Southern Observatory: www.eso.org

How Stuff Works: science.howstuffworks.com

NASA: www.nasa.gov

NASA Quest: quest.nasa.gov

www.space.com

Space Flight Now: www.spaceflightnow.com